The
WISDOM
of
ZEN

The
WISDOM
of
ZEN

Compiled by
Roger England and Anne Bancroft

ONEWORLD
OXFORD

THE WISDOM OF ZEN

Oneworld Publications
(Sales and Editorial)
185 Banbury Road
Oxford OX2 7AR
England

www.oneworld-publications.com

ISBN 1–85168–281–3

Cover and text design by Design Deluxe
Typeset by Cyclops Media Productions
Printed and bound by Graphicom Srl, Vicenza, Italy

ACKNOWLEDGEMENTS

The editors and publisher would like to thank Jasper Solomon for supplying the pictures that appear on pages v, 17, 97, 108, 121, 129, 133, 137, 145, 168 and 177. Cover image of Bodhisattva Miroku, a future Buddha, seated figure, Japan, 7th century © Copyright The British Museum. All other pictures © the editors.

CONTENTS

INTRODUCTION

PERSONAL FULFILMENT is all that seems to matter these days. If one stands back for a moment one can see how people try to fulfil themselves by pursuing love, joy, wealth, power, insight – even by dogged survival. But it also becomes clear that the more fiercely life is clutched at the faster it slips away, and the less the profound mystery of existence can be understood. Water drawn from a stream is no longer living water, for it ceases to flow. Zen holds that life, like water, cannot be grasped; people can find true fulfilment and come alive only when they give up clinging to that which is bound to pass.

So Zen is a state of liveliness and fluidity. It has no doctrine. It is based on an experience of reality to be found beyond all concepts and doctrines. In this Zen follows the understanding of the Buddha, and regards itself as faithfully portraying his insights. But although it has no doctrines, Zen does have highly stylised teaching methods and techniques of meditation. These are practised by many in the West today, with the help of teachers and Zen masters. Zen's unique contribution to spirituality is its insistence on presenting things just as they are, in all their living wonder: 'No dependence on words, but direct pointing to reality.'

So the Zen way of teaching is to demonstrate life rather than talk about it. When Zen speaks, it expresses reality not with logical explanations but in everyday conversation or with statements that so upset the hearer's presumptions as to appear like utter nonsense. Zen points to the real without distracting the seeker's attention with concepts. Sometimes Zen has to undermine deeply rooted presumptions in a drastic way, for we all hold on to comfortable ways of thinking whenever we can.

Zen's origin was in Buddhism. The Buddhist monk Bodhidharma brought Buddhism from India to China in 527 CE, one thousand years after the life of the Buddha. *Dhyana*, the Indian word meaning meditation, became *Ch'an* in China; when it reached Japan in the twelfth century it became known as Zen. *Ch'an* Buddhism developed intensely in China between the seventh and thirteenth centuries. From the fourteenth century onwards the main centre of development was Japan. Zen entered deeply into the Japanese psyche, influencing government, poetry and the arts, swordsmanship and the samurai, the tea ceremony and social gatherings.

The fundamentals of Zen have remained constant. Zen holds that Siddhartha Gautama became the Buddha, the Enlightened One, as a result of a profound spiritual experience, an immediate knowledge of reality. This perception was beyond what can be put into words and the

Buddha's verbal teaching was intended only to suggest its nature. By the brilliance of his teaching, many came to share his insight and the understanding has been passed on ever since from teacher to pupil. Because words can never convey the real message, Zen has never relied on scriptures, though it may use them as aids towards realisation.

Modern Zen is diverse, yet retains the central understanding of direct pointing. Modern teachers still demonstrate reality rather than talk about it. Useful practices from Zen's past remain in use, in particular the seemingly baffling short exchanges known as koans.

A keen and learned student called Basho came to see a Zen master. Politely the master listened as Basho expounded all the understanding of Zen he had learnt from his studies.

'You have certainly studied hard and well,' said the master. 'But all I have heard so far are words from other people. Will you now give me something of your own, from yourself?'

Basho was baffled. From himself! What could he say? The time went on and he could think of nothing. The master waited patiently and Basho could not bring forth a word. In the quiet of the garden, a frog jumped into a pond.

Introduction ⟷ xi

'Ah! The splash!' exclaimed Basho.

'That's it,' the master laughed. 'That was truly from yourself.'

Zen is a teaching to be lived rather than studied, since study can take you only part of the way. This book illustrates the methods and insights of teachers and pupils, the humour and wit of the masters, and the sharp exchanges that suddenly enlighten.

WHAT IS ZEN?

THE ORIGIN of Zen teaching is believed to have been from the Buddha, on an occasion when he was staying at Vulture Park and giving daily discourses to his followers. One morning he arrived to find twelve hundred people seated, waiting for him to speak. He sat in front of them in silence. The time went past but still there was silence. At last, silently, he held up a flower. Nobody understood this gesture except one person, who smiled, having seen that no words could be a substitute for the living flower. The Buddha said, 'Here is the true Way and I transmit it to you.' In this way he pointed out that the unmediated experience of existence – the here-and-now experience – is a profound mystical insight. The phenomenal world is seen as it is, in its 'isness', without the projection of 'I'.

ANNE BANCROFT, *Zen: Direct Pointing to Reality*

ZEN IS: being in touch with the inner workings of life
Zen is: life that knows it is worth living
Zen is: this moment speaking as time and as eternity
Zen is: seeing into the nature of things, inside and outside of myself
Zen is: when all living things of the Earth open their eyes wide and look me in the eye

FREDERICK FRANCK, *The Zen of Seeing*

*Z*EN HAS no metaphysics – Zen wishes to escape the pointless endeavour to trap life in a metaphysical net instead of simply living it.

BRUCE LEE, Striking Thoughts

*J*APANESE WRITERS generally distinguish between Zen and Zen Buddhism. The latter is a religion containing doctrine, a philosophy of life, and axioms for its practice; Zen, on the other hand, 'is'. Its whole centre is the enlightenment, or *satori*, about which no one can speak unless he himself has had the experience – and even he can say very little. It crashes upon the mind like a peal of thunder or a flash of lightning; it is 'a turning point in one's life,' 'a mental revolution,' 'a fiery baptism of spirit', but its content is inexpressible in human language. The descriptions given by Zen masters are not unlike that of the beam of ghostly light piercing the cloud of unknowing. Zen, however, is divorced from all schemes of thought, all philosophies of life, all religious dogma – according to Dr. Suzuki, it should not even be called mysticism. And since it is so divorced from all religion, it can be practised (and is practised) by people who hold no allegiance to Zen Buddhism: it is practised by a variety of people from atheists to Catholic priests.

WILLIAM JOHNSTON, *The Mysticism of the Cloud of Unknowing*

I F YOU want to understand Zen, understand it right away without deliberation, without turning your head this way or that. For while you are doing this, the object you have been seeking for is no longer there. This doctrine of immediate grasping is characteristic of Zen. Zen teaches us to go beyond logic and not to tarry even when we come up against 'the things which are not seen.'

D.T. SUZUKI, *Zen Doctrine of No Mind*

T O OPEN our hearts, to clarify our way of looking at things so that we see them freshly, vividly, clearly, without all of our hang-ups on them. To come to something and say, 'Ah, I've never seen that before.' After five days of practice, to come out and see the needles of the pine trees sparkling at you. They have been sparkling all the time. It's just you who haven't been awake enough to see that. This is Zen.

MAURINE STUART in *Meetings with Remarkable Women*, Lenore Friedman

ZEN WAS brought to China from India in 527 CE by a monk, Bodhidharma. He was received by the Emperor Wu, already a committed Buddhist, who was anxious to obtain approval for his own devout works from this renowned monk. So he asked Bodhidharma:

'I have had temples built, holy scriptures copied and ordered monks and nuns to be converted. Is there any merit, Reverend Sir, in my conduct?'

'No merit at all.'

The Emperor was taken aback by this answer. It seemed as though all he believed in was being turned upside down. He asked:

'What then is the holy truth, the first principle?'

'Vast emptiness, with nothing holy in it.'

'Who, then, are you to stand before me?'

'I do not know, your Majesty.'

D.T. SUZUKI, *Zen Doctrines of No Mind*

ZEN NEVER leaves this world of facts. Zen always lives in the midst of realities. It is not for Zen to stand apart or keep itself away from a world of names and forms.

D.T. SUZUKI, *Zen and Japanese Culture*

A SPECIAL transmission outside the Scriptures;
No dependence upon words and letters;
Direct pointing to the mind of man;
Seeing into one's own nature.

D.T. SUZUKI, *Studies in Zen*

THE WHOLE point, then, is not that Zen has no philosophy and no history, for obviously it has, but that this history and background, reflected on discursively, does not help one iota in the attainment of enlightenment which is only found by 'direct pointing at the soul'.

WILLIAM JOHNSTON, *The Still Point*

THAT THE self advances
And confirms the myriad things
Is delusion.

That the myriad things advance
And confirm the self
Is enlightenment.

DOGEN in *Studies in Zen*, D.T. Suzuki

What is Zen? ❧ 19

AFTER THE spring song, 'Vast emptiness, no holiness,'
Comes the song of snow-wind along the Yangtze River.
Late at night I too play the noteless flute of Shorin,
Piercing the mountains with its sound, the river.

L. STRYCK, *Zen: Poems, Prayers, Sermons*

AWARENESS OF Being is the secret by which people shed light on their existence, produce the power of concentration and bring wisdom to fruition. Awareness of Being is the backbone of Zen.

THICH NHAT HAHN, *Being Peace*

WHAT IS Zen? The question cannot be answered, for Zen is no 'thing' at all. It is but the Japanese name for that which is, which we and all else in existence are. There is no thing else. If we must insult supreme spirit with a definition, it is for us a state of intuitive awareness of Reality, of that one life-force which is totality in manifestation.

CHRISTMAS HUMPHREYS, *Middle Way, Spring 1979*

A boy has lost his ox, his most valuable possession, and stands alone in a vast landscape. The ox represents his real self, that which is lost sight of when we take the world at a horizontal level only and allow it no heights or depths. He has become so identified with the things of the world that he no longer sees his original nature. In fact the ox has not really gone, the boy has not really lost his true self, but he no longer has knowledge of it. He has now become aware that it is missing.

ZEN DENIES all attempts to rationalise it, make sense of it, or turn it into a philosophy, and it compares man's desire to grasp it intellectually to a finger pointing at the moon – the finger continually being mistaken for the moon itself. It has an amused indifference to the worldly goals of men. The Zen outlook has it that all is equally holy – even straw mats and horse dung – and to distinguish one of life's aspects and make it of more importance than another is to fall into dualistic error rather than reality. A famous Zen poem says:

> The perfect way knows no difficulties
> Except that it refuses to make preferences;
> Only when freed from hate and love
> It reveals itself fully and without disguise;
> A tenth of an inch's difference,
> And heaven and earth are set apart.
> If you wish to see it with your own eyes
> Have no fixed thoughts either for or against it.

ANNE BANCROFT, *Zen: Direct Pointing to Reality*

IT'S NOT so much faith in what will be, as faith in what is - this is what people lack. We have to have faith in what is now.

MASTER GUDO in *Fingers and Moons*, Trevor Leggett

SOMEONE ASKED one of the early Zen masters to teach him a way to liberation.

The Zen master said, 'Who binds you?'

The seeker of liberty said, 'No one binds me.'

The Zen master said, 'Then why seek liberation?'

'If you think there are any verbal formulations that are special mysterious secrets to be transmitted, this is not real Zen. Real Zen has no transmission. It is just a matter of people experiencing it, resulting in their ability to see each other's vision and communicate it tacitly. Over the course of centuries, Zen has branched out into different schools with individual methods, but the purpose is still the same – to point directly to the human mind.'

ANNE BANCROFT, *The Luminous Vision*

THE PRESENCE of one cell in the body implies the presence of all the others, since they cannot exist independently, separate of the others. A Vietnamese Zen master once said, 'If this speck of dust did not exist, the entire universe could not exist.' Looking at a speck of dust, an awakened person sees the universe.

THICH NHAT HANH, *The Sun Is My Heart*

ZEN TEXTS are especially demanding. The closer you get to what lies behind the imagery, the more questions they raise. The more profound one's scrutiny, the more complex the conundrums they pose. Yet everything can suddenly become simple and lucid. That extraordinary directness and simplicity can often prove stimulating. Even someone unacquainted with the higher reaches of Zen can win from an image, word or sentence an unexpected impetus to laughter which paradoxically turns at once to contemplation. Equally he may find a certain resolution, or just as easily the strange burden of a responsibility which he had previously been unaware of but now all at once rises unquenchably in him.

Authentic Zen texts allow Life to speak directly. Not the everyday life of our continual round, but the Life that we are fundamentally; the Life we ought to live outwardly, but which makes no appearance in our conscious mind or in our conscience. Basically, then, a Zen text often means something other than what we read into it at first sight. Every Zen pronouncement is a parable. But what is referred to is always the Life that lies beyond life and death.

KOSHO UCHIYAMA, *Approach to Zen*

The boy no longer wanders round in confusion searching for the ox. He begins to pay attention. He listens to teachings and looks at what he is doing. And so he comes upon the footprints of the ox. He gives a cry of joy. The ox exists, it is there somewhere.

ONE DAY I wiped out all the notions from my mind. I gave up all desire. I discarded all the words with which I thought and stayed in quietude. I felt a little queer – as if I were being carried into something, or as if I were touching some power unknown to me ... and Ztt! I entered. I lost the boundary of my physical body. I had my skin, of course, but I felt I was standing in the centre of the cosmos. I spoke, but my words had lost their meaning. I saw people coming towards me, but all were the same man. All were myself! I had never known this world. I had believed that I was created, but now I must change my opinion: I was never created; I was the cosmos; no individual Mr Sasaki existed.'

SOKEI-AN SASAKI in *Zen Notes*

WHEN AN ancient Zen master was asked about the meaning of Buddhism he replied, 'If there is any meaning in it, I myself am not liberated.' For when you have really heard the sound of rain you can hear, and see and feel, everything else in the same way – as needing no translation, as being just that which it is, though it may be impossible to say what.

ALAN WATTS in *Mystics and Sages*, Anne Bancroft

BEFORE YOU enter one of the gates of Zen, you must strip yourself of egoistic ideas. If you think you can reason out the final truth with your brain, why do you not do it? Once you begin your work in Zen, do not turn to the left nor to the right but keep going straight ahead.

NYOGEN SENZAKE, *Buddhism and Zen*

I CROSSED seas and rivers, climbed mountains, and forded streams,
In order to interview the masters, to inquire after Truth, to delve into the secrets of Zen;
And ever since I was enabled to recognise the path.
I knew that birth-and-death is not the thing I have to be concerned with.
For walking is Zen, sitting is Zen,
Whether talking or remaining silent, whether moving or standing quiet, the Essence itself is ever at ease;
Even when greeted with swords and spears it never loses its quiet way,
And all that befalls cannot perturb its serenity.

YOKO DAISHI in *Manual of Zen Buddhism*, D.T. Suzuki

YOU MUST learn to live in the present, not in the future or the past. Zen teaches that life must be seized at the moment. By living in the present you are in full contact with yourself and your environment, your energy is not dissipated and is always available. In the present there are no regrets as there are in the past. By thinking of the future, you dilute the present. The time to live is now. As long as what you are doing at the moment is *exactly* what you are doing at that moment and nothing else, you are one with yourself and with what you are doing – and that is Zen; while doing something you are doing it at the fullest.

JOE HYAMS, *Zen in the Martial Arts*

THE MOON'S the same old moon,
The flowers exactly as they were
Yet I've become the thingness
Of all the things I see!

BUNAN in *The Spiritual Journey*, Anne Bancroft

The boy has followed the footsteps a long way – he has been working at removing the obstacles in his mind. And now he can see the tail of the ox. It is almost within his reach. But first he must overcome his demanding ego, to find that which transcends it.

INNER ILLUMINATION is the whole of Zen. Zen starts with it and ends with it. When there is no illumination there is no Zen. It is not a state of mere quietude, it is not tranquillisation, it is an inner experience which has a noetic quality; there must be a certain wakening from the relative field of consciousness, a certain turning away from the ordinary form of experience which characterises our everyday life. It is a turning over at the basis of consciousness. By this the entirety of one's mental construction goes through a complete change. It's wonderful that such an insight is capable of causing such a reconstruction in one's spiritual outlook.

D.T. SUZUKI, *Studies in Zen*

PHILOSOPHERS MAY postulate reality, driving themselves to the end of the trail of logic, but none of them ever succeeds in attaining. To follow logic and believe that something *must be* is one thing, but to experience it is another.

NYOGEN SENZAKE, *Buddhism and Zen*

HOWEVER HIGH and soaring our ideas may be, we are firmly rooted in the earth; there is no way of escaping from physical existence. Whatever thoughts we may have must be related to our body, if they are to influence life in any way. The monk is asked to solve highly abstract metaphysical problems; and to do this he devotes himself to meditation. But as long as this meditation remains abstract there will be no practical solution. The Yogin may think that he understands this clearly; but as long as this understanding is restricted to his hours of meditation and he does not put it into practice in his daily life, the solution remains in the realm of ideas, bears no fruit and soon dies out. Zen masters have, therefore, always been anxious to see their monks work hard on the farm and in the woods or mountains. In fact they would themselves lead the working party, taking up the spade, the cutters, or the axe, carrying water or pulling the hand-cart.

SOHAKU OGATA, *Zen for the West*

MY ADVICE to those whose eyes have not yet been opened to the truth – leap from the net and see how immense is the ocean.

L. STRYCK, *Zen: Poems, Prayers, Sermons*

NANSEN WAS once asked by Joshu, 'What is the Way?'
Nansen: 'Ordinary mind is the Way.'
Joshu: 'Are we to try to get it?'
Nansen: 'As soon as one tries to get it, one deviates from it.'
Joshu: 'How do we know it without trying?'
Nansen: 'The Way is beyond both knowing and not-knowing. Knowing is false perceiving and not-knowing is the lack of awareness. When one attains to the way, which is beyond doubt, one will see it as clearly as one sees the vastness of the universe. What then is the use of arguing about it?'

SOHAKU OGATA, *Zen for the West*

THE HIGHEST principle cannot be explained;
It is neither free nor bound.
Lively and attuned to everything,
It is always right before you.

NIU T'OU in *Buddhism and Zen*, Nyogen Senzake

CLARITY AND EMPTINESS

AT THE north window, icy drafts whistle through the
    cracks,
At the south pond, wild geese huddle in snowy reeds,
Above, the mountain moon is pinched thin with cold,
Freezing clouds threaten to plunge from the sky.
Buddhas might descend to this world by the thousands,
They couldn't add or subtract one thing.

HAKUIN in *Studies in the Lankavatara Sutra*, D.T. Suzuki

NAN-IN a Japanese master received a university professor,
full of learning and talk, who came to inquire about Zen.
Nan-in served tea. He poured his visitor's cup full, and
then kept on pouring.

The professor watched the overflow until he no longer could
restrain himself. 'It is overfull. No more will go in.'

'Like this cup,' Nan-in said, 'you are full of your own opinions
and speculations. How can I show you Zen unless you first
empty your cup?'

R.H. BLYTH, *Zen in English Literature*

WHY, IT'S but the motion of eyes and brows!
And here I've been seeking it far and wide.
Awakened at last, I find the moon
Above the pines, the river surging high.

YTJISHUN in *Zen: Poems, Prayers, Sermons, Anecdotes, Interviews*, L. Stryck

A SUDDEN CONCENTRATION of attention on a rainy August morning. Clusters of bright red berries, some wrinkled, some blemished, others perfect, hanging among green leaves. The experience could not have lasted more than a few seconds, but that was a moment out of time. I was caught up in what I saw: I became a part of it: the berries, the leaves, the raindrops and I, we were all of a piece. A moment of beauty and harmony and meaning. A moment of understanding.

RALPH HEATHERINGTON in *Quaker Faith and Practice*

MASTER RINZAI said: 'When hungry, I eat; when tired, I sleep. Fools laugh at me. The wise understand.'

D.T. SUZUKI, *Essays in Zen Buddhism*

I F YOU fail to achieve emancipation in this life, when do you expect to achieve it? While still alive, you should be tireless in practising contemplation. The practice consists of abandonments. 'The abandonment of what?' you may ask. You should abandon all the workings of your relative consciousness, which you have been cherishing since eternity; retire within your inner being and see the reason of it. As your self-reflection grows deeper and deeper, the moment will surely come upon you when the spiritual flower will suddenly burst into bloom, illuminating the entire universe.

WU-HSIN in *Studies in the Lankavatara Sutra*, D.T. Suzuki

T HE PRICE of being able to find this 'other' as a living wisdom within myself had been that I must want nothing from it, I must turn to it with complete acceptance of what is, expecting nothing, wanting to change nothing; and it was only then that I received those illuminating flashes which had been most important in shaping my life.

MARION MILNER in *Weavers of Wisdom*, Anne Bancroft

Now the boy has found the ox and has put a rope round it to stop it getting away again. But it gives him a lot of trouble, kicking and jumping about. He has used the rope of intellect and concept, thinking he has caught the ox by understanding it with his mind. He compares it to what others have told him. But it is unique, no knowledge about it can tether it.

THE PURE lotus growing in muddy water is a metaphor for enlightenment. The lotus arises from all its impediments. It actually needs the impurity of the water for its nourishment. In the same way, in our personal development, we can't just work with what we like about ourselves. We have to work with our muddy water. We have to work with our problems and our hang-ups because that's where the action is.

BERNARD GLASSMAN, *Instructions to the Cook*

MASTER TANKA, staying in a temple in mid-winter, used one of the wooden Buddha images to make a fire. The temple monk came running in: 'What are you doing?'

'Burning up a wooden statue.'

'But it's a Buddha!'

Stirring up the ashes, Master Tanka asked, 'Can you see any of the reliquary stones supposed to remain in the ashes of saints?'

'How can you expect to find reliquary stones in a wooden statue?' asked the scandalised monk.

'Oh well, if that's the case,' said Master Tanka, 'may I have another one to keep me warm?'

IRMGARD SCHLOEGL, *The Wisdom of the Zen Masters*

JOSHU ASKED Nansen: 'What is the path?'

Nansen said: 'Everyday life is the path.'

Joshu asked: 'Can it be studied?'

Nansen said: 'If you try to study, you will be far away from it.'

Joshu asked: 'If I do not study, how can I know it is the path?'

Nansen said: 'If you want to reach the true path beyond doubt, place yourself in the same freedom as sky. You name it neither good nor not-good.'

At these words Joshu was enlightened.

TREVOR LEGGETT, *The Old Zen Master*

IT WAS beyond description and altogether incommunicable, for there was nothing in the world to which it could be compared ... As I looked round and up and down, the whole universe with its multitudinous sense-objects now appeared quite different; what was loathsome before, together with ignorance and passions, was seen to be nothing else but the outflow of my own inmost nature, which in itself remained bright, true and transparent.

HAKUIN in *Spiritual Journey*, Anne Bancroft

MASTER HUI-NENG got enlightenment by listening to the chanting of the Diamond Sutra, Master Teshan got it by observing that Master Lung-t'an blew a candle flame out, Master Ling-yun got it by seeing a peach flower falling, Master Po-chang got it when his master Ma-tsu twisted his nose in his young days, Master Hakuin got it by hearing the sound of the temple gong. About enlightenment little can be said that will even remotely express the reality. It is a great crash accompanied by joy and followed by deep peace. It has been poetically compared to the smashing of a layer of ice or the pulling down of a crystal tower; or the clouds have parted and the bright sun pierces through – others will say that it is as though their skull were broken into a thousand pieces.

WILLIAM JOHNSTON, *The Still Point*

ALL PEOPLE have their own living road to heaven. Until they walk on this road, they are like drunkards who cannot tell which way is which. Then when they set foot on this road and lose their confusion, it is up to them which way they shall go – they are no longer subject to the arbitrary directions of others.

SOKEI-AN SASAKI in *Zen Notes*

The boy can now lead the ox with a loose rein. It has taken a lot of time and trouble but now it is meek and faithful. He has had to live the truth for a long time before all the intellectual concepts died away. But now he and the ox are in harmony.

THERE IS no here, no there. Infinity is before our eyes.

SENG T'SAN in *Studies in the Lankavatara Sutra*, D.T. Suzuki

IF YOU have developed great capacity and cutting insight, you can undertake Zen right where you are. Without getting it from another, you understand clearly on your own.

The penetrating spiritual light and vast open tranquility have never been interrupted since beginningless time. The pure, uncontrived, ineffable, complete true mind does not act as a partner to objects of material sense, and is not a companion of myriad things.

When the mind is always as clear and bright as ten suns shining together, detached from views and beyond feelings, cutting through the ephemeral illusions of birth and death, this is what is meant by the saying, 'Mind itself is Buddha.'

You do not have to abandon worldly activities in order to attain effortless unconcern. You should know that worldly activities and effortless unconcern are not two different things – but if you keep thinking about rejection and grasping, you make them into two.

HUI NENG in *The Luminous Vision*, Anne Bancroft

AWAKENING IS where there is no birth, no extinction; it is seeing into the state of Suchness, absolutely transcending all the categories constructed by mind.

LANKAVATARA SUTRA in *The Perennial Philosophy*, A. Huxley

YOU DO not need paraphernalia, practices, or realisations to attain it. What you need to do is to clean out the influences of the psychological afflictions connected with the external world that have been accumulating in your psyche since beginningless time.

Make your mind as wide open as cosmic space; detach from graspings in the conceptual consciousness, and false ideas and imaginings will also be like empty space. Then this effortless subtle mind will naturally be unimpeded wherever it turns.

JOHN BLOFELD, *The Zen Teaching of Huang Po*

WITH THE lamp of word and discrimination one must go beyond word and discrimination and enter upon the path of realisation.

D.T. SUZUKI, *Studies in the Lankavatara Sutra*

Clarity and Emptiness

THERE WAS a blackbird in the garden, and it was as though there had never been a blackbird before. All my inner turmoil melted away and I felt full of clarity and inner peace. I seemed at one with everything around me and saw people with all judgement suspended, so that they seemed perfect in themselves.

ANNE BANCROFT, *Zen: Direct Pointing to Reality*

HUMAN LIVES go along with circumstances. It is not necessary to reject activity and seek quiet; just make yourself inwardly empty while outwardly harmonious. Then you will be at peace in the midst of frenetic activity in the world.

SOKEI-AN SASAKI in *Zen Notes*

ZEN ENLIGHTENMENT is as if you have been away from home for many years, when you suddenly see your father in town. You know him right away, without a doubt. There is no need to ask anyone else whether he is your father or not.

DOGEN in *A Primer of Soto Zen*, Reiho Masanuga

THE TRUTH is the most obvious thing, yet we are always looking for a needle in a haystack. When you see the Truth, nothing changes. A tree is still a tree, a mountain is a mountain. As Maezumi Roshi once said, 'I can't believe all the suffering and frustration people go through only to realise that a table is a table, a chair is a chair.'

K. DURCKHEIM, *The Grace of Zen*

DAY AND night the cold wind blows through my robe.
In the forest, only fallen leaves;
Wild chrysanthemums can no longer be seen.
Next to my hermitage there is an ancient bamboo grove;
Never changing, it awaits my return.

JOHN STEVENS, *One Robe, One Bowl*

AT ONE stroke I forgot all my knowledge!
There's no use for artificial discipline,
For, move as I will, I manifest the ancient Way.

HAKUIN in *Zen: Direct Pointing to Reality*, Anne Bancroft

I TOOK A walk. Suddenly I stood still, filled with the realisation that I had no body or mind. All I could see was one great illuminating Whole – omnipresent, perfect, lucid and serene. It was like an all-embracing mirror from which the mountains and rivers of the earth were projected … I felt clear and transparent.

HAN-SHAN in *On Having No Head*, D.E. Harding

LIKE THE empty sky it has no boundaries,
Yet it is right in this place, ever profound and clear.
When you seek to know it, you cannot see it.
You cannot take hold of it,
But you cannot lose it.
In not being able to get it, you get it.
When you are silent, it speaks;
When you speak, it is silent.
The great gate is wide open to bestow alms,
And no crowd is blocking the way.

TAKUAN in *Essays in Zen Buddhism I*, D.T. Suzuki

ALL OF a sudden you find your mind and body wiped out of existence. This is what is known as letting go your hold. As you regain your breath it is like drinking water and knowing it is cold. It is joy inexpressible.

HAKUIN in *On Having No Head*, D.E. Harding

THOSE WHO, reflecting within themselves,
Testify to the truth of Self-nature,
To the truth that Self-nature is no-nature,
Have gone beyond all sophistry.
For them opens the gate of the oneness of cause and
     effect,
And straight runs the path of non-duality and
     non-trinity.
Abiding with the not-particular which is in particulars,
Whether going or returning, they remain forever
     unmoved;
Taking hold of the no-thought which is in thoughts,
In every act of theirs they hear the voice of the truth.

SOHAKU OGATA, *Zen for the West*

The boy plays his flute as he rides the ox home. He is out in the clear sunlight. But the ox is still in the picture, it is still separate from him even if the two are together. He still thinks of his original nature conceptually, as 'out there'.

WHATEVER DOUBTS and indecisions I had before were completely dissolved like a piece of thawing ice. I called out loudly, 'How wondrous! How wondrous! There is no birth and death from which one has to escape, nor is there any supreme knowledge after which one has to strive!'

KU-MEI YU in *Spiritual Journey*, Anne Bancroft

WHENCE IS my life?
Whither does it go?
I sit alone in my hut,
And meditate quietly;
With all my thinking I know no where,
Nor do I come to any whither:
Such is my present,
Eternally changing – all in Emptiness!
In this Emptiness the Ego rests for a while,
With its yeas and nays;
I know not where to set them up,
I follow my Karma as it moves, with perfect contentment.

SOHAKU OGATA, *Zen for the West*

ZEN IS a matter of experience and not of mere concept or thought. Zen therefore avoids taking any system of thought as its own or as the standard of its life.

SOHAKU OGATA, *Zen for the West*

THE KOAN I ordinarily give my pupils is: 'All things return to the One; where does the One return?' I make them search after this. To search after it means to awaken a great, inquiring spirit for the ultimate meaning of the koan. The manyness of things returns to One, but where does the One finally return? I say to them: Make this inquiry with all the strength that lies in your personality, giving yourself no time to relax in this effort. In whatever physical position you are, and in whatever business you are employed, never pass your time idly. Where does the One finally return? Try to press your spirit of inquiry forward, steadily and uninterruptedly. When your searching spirit comes to this stage, the time has come for your spiritual flower to burst out.

KAO-FENG in *Ch'an and Zen Teaching, Series 2*, Lu K'uan Yu

ONE STROKE has made me forget all my previous
  knowledge,
No artificial discipline is needed;
In every movement I uphold the ancient way,
And never fall into the rut of quietism;
No traces are left where I walk
And my senses are not fettered by rules of conduct;
Everywhere all those who have attained to the truth,
Declare this to be of the highest order.

SOHAKU OGATA, *Zen for the West*

ALL BEINGS and things are not separate from the true-nature.
The characteristic of this true-nature is simply 'it is'. And
because this nature cannot be added to or taken away
from it's the same in all of us. There is not more in a clever
person or less in an ordinary person. This nature encompasses
limitless space and when you see the perfection of this nature,
that seeing purifies your vision. When your visual sense-base is
purified then your other senses become purified too and the
entire world is transformed.

MASTER KU SAN in *Spiritual Journey*, Anne Bancroft

Clarity and Emptiness ↝ 51

FOR EXAMPLE, I talked about this before but, the power which makes my heart beat, sends blood flowing through my whole body, and allows me to breathe so many times per minute, is not something which I control or activate. The power which does these things works completely beyond my thoughts. But because this power comes from beyond my thoughts, can we say this power is not I? As long as this power is working in me, it is indeed the reality of my life. It's not only these kind of physical functions, but the same is true for the ideas and thoughts which arise in my head, too. Looking at the contents of these ideas and thoughts, it certainly appears as though they are my thoughts and ideas. But it must be said that the very power which allows me to work out these thoughts and ideas, is a transcendent power beyond my thoughts. However, even if I say that this power is a transcendent power beyond my thoughts, it's no mistake that as long as it is actually working in me, it is the reality of the life of the self.

KOSHO UCHIYAMA ROSHI, *Approach to Zen*

IN THE very ultimate,
Rules and standards do not exist.
Develop a mind of equanimity,
And all deeds are put to rest.
Anxious doubts are completely cleared.

Seng Ts'an in *Buddhism and Zen*, Nyogen Senzake

IF ALL things are to be returned to the One, to where is that One to be returned?

Chao Choo in *Zen Dictionary*, Ernest Wood

ENLIGHTENMENT MEANS seeing through to your own essential nature, and this at the same time means seeing through to the essential nature of the cosmos and of all things. For seeing through to essential nature is the wisdom of enlightenment. One may call essential nature truth if one wants to. In Buddhism, from ancient times, it has been called suchness or the one Mind. In Zen it has also been called nothingness, or one's original face. The designations may be different but the content is completely the same.

Master Yasutani in *Zen Enlightenment*, H. Dumoulin

Clarity and Emptiness ❧ 53

MOST OF us avoid the real purpose of life, because it is always in our nature to anticipate; we dream of something else, something more. The dream arises from habitual discontent. So we roam about, motivated by the unconscious and fixed idea that we dislike ourselves as we are and that we must be better. In fact, there is no such thing as 'better'.

TREVOR LEGGETT, *The Old Zen Master*

SUDDENLY A great doubt manifested itself before me. It was as though I were frozen solid in the midst of an ice sheet extending tens of thousands of miles. A purity filled my breast and I could neither go forward nor retreat. To all intents and purposes I was out of my mind and the koan 'Mu' alone remained ... This state lasted for several days. Then I chanced to hear the sound of the temple bell and I was suddenly transformed. It was as if a sheet of ice had been smashed ... and I returned to my senses. All my former doubts vanished ... and in a loud voice I called: 'Wonderful, wonderful. There is no cycle of birth and death through which one must pass. There is no enlightenment one must seek.'

HAKUIN in *Crazy Clouds*, Perle Besserman

TRUE EMPTINESS – that which is beyond concepts and words – is sometimes called 'suchness' or 'thusness'. It means 'it is so'. It can only be directly experienced. If you want to know what an orange is like, you have to taste it. Then you enter the suchness of an orange or the suchness of the sea. In Zen, the very beingness of our life is its suchness. To know that beingness you must experience it without concepts.

DOGEN in *Manual of Zen Buddhism*, D.T. Suzuki

LOOK INTO the serenity of mind to which all things return;

Realise that the world of particulars exists because of the One Mind;

Observe the perfect and mysterious interpenetration of all things;

Observe that there is nothing but Suchness;

Observe that the mirror of consciousness reflects the images of all things, which thereby do not obstruct each other;

Observe that, when one particular object is picked up, all the others are picked up with it.

MASTER FA-TSANG in *Spiritual Journey*, Anne Bancroft

The boy has reached home. And when he is truly home, he sees that the ox has gone. But he is unconcerned, for he now knows the ox was no other than himself. He is at home in himself and the ox is no longer separate. There is no more searching. But he himself is still in the picture.

TO SET up what you like against what you dislike –
This is the disease of the mind;
When the deep meaning of the Way is not understood
Peace of mind is disturbed to no purpose.
The Way is perfect like unto vast space,
With nothing wanting, nothing superfluous;
It is indeed due to making choice
That its suchness is lost sight of.

In the higher realm of true Suchness
There is neither self nor other;
When direct identification is sought,
We can only say, 'Not two.'
The two exist because of the One,
But hold not even to this One;
When a mind is not disturbed,
The ten thousand things offer no offence.

SENG T'SAN in *Studies in the Lankavatara Sutra*, D.T. Suzuki

A MAN CAME to Zen Master Ikkyu.

'Master, please write for me some words of highest wisdom.' Ikkyu took his brush and wrote one word: 'Attention'. 'Is that all?' asked the man. 'Please add something more.' Ikkyu wrote: 'Attention. Attention.' 'Well,' said the man, 'I don't see much depth or subtlety in that.' Ikkyu then wrote: 'Attention. Attention. Attention.' Angrily the man, who thought he was being made a fool of, demanded, 'What does that word "Attention" mean anyway?' Ikkyu answered, 'Attention means attention.'

Comment by Philip Kapleau: 'For the ordinary man, whose mind is a checkerboard of criss-crossing reflections, opinions and prejudices, bare attention is virtually impossible; his life is thus centred not on reality itself but in his ideas of it. By focusing the mind wholly on each object and every action, zazen strips it of extraneous thoughts and allows us to enter into a full rapport with life.'

P. KAPLEAU, *The Three Pillars of Zen*

UMMON BUNEN wanted his followers to be very clear and definite in what they were doing, and to illustrate this said: 'When you sit, sit; when you walk, walk. Above all, don't wobble.'

ERNEST WOOD, *Zen Dictionary*

AS LONG as people are beguiled by words, they can never expect to penetrate to the heart of Zen. Why? Because words are merely a vehicle on which the truth is carried. Not understanding the meaning of the old masters and their koans, people try to find it in the words only, but they will find nothing there to lay their hands on. The truth itself is beyond all description, but it is by words that the truth is manifested. Let us, then, forget the words when we gain the truth itself. This is done only when we have an insight through experience into that which is indicated by the words. When T'ung-shan was asked, 'What is the Buddha?' he answered, 'Three rolls of flax.' Such an answer is like the royal thoroughfare to the capital: when you are once on it, every step you take is in the right direction.

LU K'UAN YU, *Ch'an and Zen Teaching, Series 1*

NO LOVE and no hatred: that is enough.
Understanding can come,
Spontaneously clear
As daylight in a cave.

SHIN JIN MEI in *The Zen Way to the Martial Arts*, Taisen
Deshimaru

THE PURPOSE of going to abandoned, grassy places and doing
zazen is to search for our self-nature. Now, at this moment,
where is your self-nature? When you have attained your
self-nature, you can free yourself from birth and death. How
would you free yourself when you are about to die? When you
have freed yourself from birth and death, you will know where to
go. After your death, where do you go?

TOSOTSU JUETSU in *Crazy Clouds*, Perle Besserman

MEDITATION AND ZAZEN

SILENCE IS an art we in the twenty-first century have pretty much lost. But silence is the shaft we descend to the depths of contemplation. Silence is the vehicle that takes us to the innermost centre of our being, which is the place for all authentic experience.

How do we practise the Way of silence? The core of Zen practice is zazen, or sitting meditation. Zazen is a discipline in which we silence and harmonise the body and mind and breath, which acts first of all therapeutically, and eventually, when all things are ready, effects a specific spiritual experience.

ELAINE MCINNES, *Roshi*

PEOPLE WHO study Buddhism should seek real, true perception and understanding. If you attain real, true perception and understanding, birth and death don't affect you – you are free to go or stay. You needn't seek wonders, for wonders come of themselves.

Just put thoughts to rest and don't seek outwardly anymore. When things come up, then give them your attention; just trust what is functional in you at present, and you have nothing to be concerned about.

SOKEI-AN SASAKI in *Zen Notes*

THE OBJECT of Zen training consists in making us realise that Zen is our daily experience and not something put in from the outside. A master, Dogo, had a novice called Soshin. When Soshin first came to the monastery, it was natural for him to expect lessons in Zen from his teacher. But Dogo gave him no special lessons and this bewildered and disappointed Soshin. One day he said to Dogo:

'It's some time since I came here, but not a word has been given me regarding the essence of Zen teaching.'

Dogo replied, 'Since your arrival I have been giving you lessons all the time on the matter of Zen discipline.'

'What kind of lesson could it have been?'

'When you bring me a cup of tea in the morning, I take it; when you serve me a meal, I accept it; when you bow to me, I return it with a nod. How else do you expect to be taught the understanding of Zen?'

Soshin hung his head, pondering these puzzling words.

Dogo said, 'If you want to see, see right at once. When you begin to think, you miss the point.'

LU K'UAN YU, *Ch'an and Zen Teaching, Series 2*

DON'T DESPISE afflictions, just purify your mind. Laying hold of the mind means judging if the mind is in a proper state or not. It is like taking a lamp into a dark cave where sunlight or moonlight has never come in; the old darkness doesn't go outside, but suddenly it becomes light inside. With the light of wisdom, the darkness of ignorance and affliction don't have to go away to be gone. At night the sky is dark, but when the sunlight comes out, the sky becomes daylight. The mind is also like this; illusion is darkness, enlightenment is light – when the light of wisdom shines, the darkness of afflictions suddenly turns light. Enlightenment is not something separate.

Your own light of wisdom is clear and bright of itself, but when obscured by false ideas you lose this, and therefore create illusions. It is like when someone dreams; whatever it is seems to appear real, but after awakening there is not a single thing. Dreamlike illusions are seen to be originally non-existent once you have awakened.

THOMAS CLEARY, *The Original Face*

THE BLUE mountains are of themselves blue mountains;
The white clouds are of themselves white clouds

R.H. BLYTH, *Zen in English Literature*

WE ARE still called upon to wrestle with the curious phenomenon of the complex human self, needed but excessive, which resists letting the world in. Meditation practice gives us a way to scrape, soften, tan it. The intent of the koan theme is to provide the student with a brick to knock on the gate, to get through and beyond that first barrier.

CLAUDE WHITMYER, *Mindfulness and Meaningful Work*

GREAT DOUBT: great awakening.
Little doubt: little awakening.
No doubt: no awakening.

These terse lines express how penetration of the mysterious is directly related to the degree and intensity of questioning. Doubt or questioning is seen as the indispensable key to awakening. It is the vitality of a meditative attitude, the driving force which heightens the sense of the mysterious to the point where it unexpectedly reveals what until then had remained withdrawn and unsuspected.

S. BATCHELOR, *The Faith to Doubt*

THE BUDDHA spent the rainy period practising the meditation of mindfulness on the in and the out breath. 'It was in this way that mindfully I breathed in and mindfully I breathed out. When breathing a long breath, I knew that it was long; and when breathing it out I knew "I breathe out a long breath". The same with the short breath, knowing it to be entering and knowing it to be leaving. In mindfulness I was conscious of the entire process.

'In this way also I practised contemplation on the body. When standing, I was aware that I was standing; when sitting, there was total knowledge of sitting; and when lying down, the full experience of lying down. By experiencing each moment, my mind clung no more to the world.

'The mindfulness of in and out breathing, of body contemplation, of keeping consciousness of the moment, is a noble occupation and a sublime way, leading to independence of mind and to wisdom.'

ANNE BANCROFT, *The Buddha Speaks*

I AM ALWAYS saying we must concentrate 'here and now,' create 'here and now.' That way, we become fresh, new. Yesterday's zazen is not the same as today's.

TAISEN DESHIMARU, *The Zen Way to the Martial Arts*

POSTURE IS basic to the practice of zazen. Basically, your posture is the expression of your Buddha nature. How clearly and with what feeling of reverence for your life, you sit upon this cushion! It's a wonderful feeling, to just *sit*. And to take a deep breath and feel every pore of you come alive right out to the ends of your hair and your toenails and scalp and cheeks – everything coming alive. It is imperative to have good posture for this experience. Otherwise your breath cannot go through you.

This is a practice on this earth, not out in space somewhere. You're right here, on this wonderful planet, your knees are solidly planted on the ground. From there you grow. Your spine like the stem of a flower, your head like a blossom on top of it. And everything in wonderful, clear alignment. Then you regulate your breath: let it fill you up, let it slowly out, then let your breath breathe you.

MAURINE STUART in *Meetings with Remarkable Women*,
L. Friedman

NO AMOUNT of calculating thought can solve the paradoxical koans of the Zen tradition. Koans call for an alternative approach. They astonish and perplex: they point to a mystery, not to a problem. They are like mirrors which can reflect the untapped depths of human experience. It is futile to

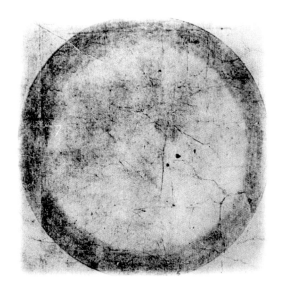

Now at last the boy too has gone from the picture and it is just an empty circle, the circle that has contained the last seven pictures. There is no more duality. But the final goal is not quite here.

examine them with the conventional tools of analysis and reason. One has to look at them in an altogether different *way*. As you probe them and turn them, gaze at and listen to them, they may suddenly reveal a hitherto unrealised intuition of their meaning.

S. BATCHELOR, *The Faith to Doubt*

To ONE who practises Zen any such term as 'holy' or 'Buddha' is a trap, implying the reality of such things when in fact they only exist as concepts in the mind. Zen masters, when they met each other, would rock with laughter at the idea that they were supposed to be holy and worthy of reverence and would often caricature each other in portrait form as rotund or absurdly wizened old men, with such titles as 'a bag of rice' or 'a snowflake in a hot oven'. They would delightedly set traps, trying to trick each other into conceptual statements about enlightenment or Buddhism or Nirvana, and burst into laughter when the trap was subtly acknowledged or avoided.

ANNE BANCROFT, *Zen: Direct Pointing to Reality*

FATHER WILLIAM Johnston, a Jesuit, went to meditate in a Japanese Zen monastery. After sitting in meditation for some time his legs began to ache terribly. The master gave him advice on this and then asked him what practice he was following in his meditation. Johnston replied that he was sitting silently in the presence of God without words or thoughts or images or ideas. The master asked if his God was everywhere, and when he replied yes, asked if he was 'wrapped around in God'. The answer was again yes.

'And you experience this?' asked the master.

'Yes.'

'Very good, very good,' said the master, 'continue this way. Just keep on. And eventually you will find that God will disappear and only Johnston remain.'

Johnston was shocked by this remark because it sounded like a denial of all that he had thought of as sacred. He decided to contradict the master and said, smilingly, 'God will not disappear. But Johnston might well disappear and only God be left.'

'Yes, yes,' the master answered, smiling, 'It's the same thing. That is what I mean.'

ANNE BANCROFT, *Zen: Direct Pointing to Reality*

ZEN STUDENTS are with their masters at least ten years before they presume to teach others. Nan-in was visited by Tenno, who, having passed his apprenticeship, had become a teacher. The day happened to be rainy, so Tenno wore wooden clogs and carried an umbrella. After greeting him Nan-in remarked:

'I suppose you left your wooden clogs in the vestibule. I want to know if your umbrella is on the right or left side of the clogs.'

Tenno, confused, had no instant answer. He realised that he was unable to carry his Zen every minute. He became Nan-in's pupil, and he studied six more years to accomplish his every-minute Zen.

PAUL REPS, *Zen Flesh, Zen Bones*

WHEN MU-CHOU was asked, 'We dress and eat every day, and how do we escape from having to put on clothes and eat food?' he answered, 'We dress; we eat.'

'I don't understand,' said the monk.

'If you don't understand, put on your clothes and eat your food.'

LU K'UAN YU, *Ch'an and Zen Teaching, Series 2*

WHEN YOU contemplate the body by being within the body, you should not engage in all sorts of ideas about it; the same when you contemplate feelings by being within feelings, you should enter in without ideas; the same applies to contemplating the mind by being within the mind and contemplating thoughts by being within thoughts. The thoughts should be just the objects of mind and you should not apply yourself to any train of ideas connected with them. In this way, by putting ideas aside, your mind will become tranquil and steady. It will enter into a meditation that is without discursive thought and is rapturous and joyful.

ANNE BANCROFT, *The Buddha Speaks*

BOTH TAKUAN and Bankei stressed the fact that the 'original' or 'unborn' mind is constantly working miracles even in the most ordinary person. Even though a tree has innumerable leaves, the mind takes them in all at once without being 'stopped' by any one of them. Explaining this to a visiting monk, Bankei said, 'To prove that your mind is the Buddha mind, notice how all that I say here goes into you without missing a single thing, even though I don't try to push it into you.'

ANNE BANCROFT, *The Spiritual Journey*

WHILE SUBTLY aware of all circumstances, you are empty and have no subjective stance towards them. Like the breeze in the pines, the moon in the water, there is a clear and light harmony. You have no coming and going mind, and you do not linger over appearances.

The essence is in being inwardly open and accommodating while outwardly responsive without unrest. Be like spring causing the flowers to bloom, like a mirror reflecting images, and you will naturally emerge, aloof of all tumult.

SOKEI-AN SASAKI in *Zen Notes*

LOOK UPON the body as unreal
An image in a mirror, the reflection of the moon in water
Contemplate the mind as formless
Yet bright and pure

Not a single thought arising
Empty, yet perceptive, still, yet illuminating
Complete like the Great Emptiness
Containing all that is wonderful

HAN SHAN TE CH'ING in *Buddhism and Zen*, Nyogen Senzake

IN BUDDHISM there is a word which means wishlessness or aimlessness. The idea is that we do not put anything ahead of ourselves and run after it. When we practice sitting meditation, we sit just to enjoy the sitting. We do not sit in order to become enlightened, a buddha, or anything else. Each moment we sit brings us back to life, and there we sit in a way that we enjoy sitting the entire time. Walking meditation is the same. We do not try to arrive anywhere. We take peaceful, happy steps, and we enjoy them. If we think of the future – of what we want to realise – or if we think of the past – our many regrets – we will lose our steps, and that would be a pity … This is an exercise in the art of living. Everything we do can be like this. Whether we are planting lettuce, washing dishes, writing a poem, or adding columns of numbers, it is not different from this. All of these things are on an equal footing … I myself am a poet. One day an American scholar told me, 'Don't waste your time gardening, growing lettuce. You can write more poems instead. Not many people write poems the way you do, but anyone can grow lettuce.' That is not my way of thinking. I know very well that if I do not grow lettuce, I cannot write poems. Eating a tangerine, washing dishes, and growing lettuce in mindfulness are essential to me to write poetry.

THICH NHAT HANH, *The Heart of Understanding*

O N BEING asked how to escape from the 'heat', another master directed the questioner to the place where it is neither hot nor cold. When asked to explain himself he replied, 'In summer we sweat; in winter we shiver.' Or, as a poem puts it:

When cold, we gather round the hearth before the blazing fire;
When hot, we sit on the bank of the mountain stream in the bamboo grove.

ALAN WATTS, *The Way of Zen*

W HEN TALKING about zazen, I like to use the metaphor of the moon and the lake. Our thoughts and emotions are like the ripples and waves that disturb the reflective surface of the lake, so that we can't see the moon. Of course the moon is always there, even if we can't see it, and it's also important to see the ripples. But we still need to see the moon clearly to know that it's there. So in meditation, when we let the ripples of our thoughts and the waves of our emotions settle, it's as if we've cleared the lake so the moon can appear.

BERNARD GLASSMAN, *Instructions to the Cook*

THE INTENTION of all Zen devices, states, sayings, and expressions is in their ability to hook the seeker. The only important thing is liberation – people should not be attached to the means.

THOMAS MERTON, *Mystics and Zen Masters*

POUR OUT everything that has accumulated in your mind – what you have learned or heard, false understanding, clever or witty sayings, the so-called truth of Zen, Buddha's teachings, self-conceit, arrogance and so on. Concentrate on the koan, which you have not yet understood. That is to say, cross your legs firmly, hold your spine straight, and paying no attention to the time of day, keep up your concentration until like a living corpse you grow unaware of your whereabouts, of east, west, south and north. The mind moves in response to the outside world and knows when it is touched. The time will come when all thoughts cease to stir and there will be no working of consciousness. Then all of a sudden you smash your brain to pieces and for the first time realise that the truth is in your own possession and has been from the very beginning. Would not this be a great satisfaction to you in your daily life?

SOHAKU OGATA *Zen for the West*

In this picture there are clouds and plum trees and everything is just as it is. Grass is growing by itself and water flows down. Everything in the universe is imbued with divine nature. The world is alive in a way it wasn't before. Each thing appears to the boy in its Suchness.

THE VARIOUS teachings and techniques of buddhas and Zen masters are only set forth so that you will individually step back into yourself, understand your own original mind and see your own original nature, so that you reach a state of great rest, peace, and happiness.

SOHAKU OGATA, *Zen for the West*

WHEN T'UNG-SHAN was asked, 'What is the Buddha?' he answered, 'Three rolls of flax.' Such an answer is like the royal thoroughfare to the capital, when you are once on it, every step you take is in the right direction.

D.T. Suzuki, *Manual of Zen Buddhism*

SITTING QUIETLY, doing nothing,
Spring comes, and the grass grows by itself.

R.H. BLYTH, *Zen in English Literature*

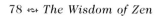

JOSHU WAS once asked by a monk, 'What is the meaning of the Patriarch's coming from the West?'
Joshu: 'The oak tree in the garden.'

Words do not represent facts,
Statements mislead for catching the point.
Those who follow words lose their lives,
Those trapped by statements get lost.

SOHAKU OGATA, *Zen for the West*

THERE IS a meditation called the meditation on the miraculousness of existence. 'Existence' means being in the present. 'The miraculousness of existence' means to be aware that the universe is contained in each thing, and that the universe could not exist if it did not contain each thing. This awareness of interconnectedness, interpenetration, and interbeing makes it impossible for us to say something 'is' or 'is not,' so we call it 'miraculous existence.'

THICH NHAT HANH, *The Sun Is My Heart*

WHEN HECKLED by an aggressive Nichiren monk who kept insisting that he couldn't understand a word, Bankei asked him to come closer. The monk stepped forward. 'Closer still', said Bankei. The monk came forward again. 'How well you understand me!' said Bankei.

ANNE BANCROFT, *The Spiritual Journey*

KATO-DEWANOKAMI-YASUOKI, lord of Osu in the province of Iyo, was passionate about the military arts. One day the great master Bankei called on him and, as they sat face to face, the young lord grasped his spear and made as if to pierce Bankei. But the master silently flicked its head aside with his rosary and said, 'No good. You're too worked up.'

Years later Yasuoki, who had become a great spearsman, spoke of Bankei as the one who had taught him most about the art.

L. STRYCK, *Zen: Poems, Prayers, Sermons, Anecdotes, Interviews*

EVERY DAY the monk Baso sat in zazen.

Watching him, Master Nangaku asked: 'What are you trying to attain by sitting?'

'I am trying to become a Buddha.'

Thereupon Nangaku picked up a bit of roof tile and began grinding it on a rock in front of him.

'What are you doing, Master?' asked Baso.

'I am polishing it to make a mirror.'

'How could polishing a tile make a mirror?'

'How could sitting in zazen make a Buddha?'

'What should I do, then?'

Nangaku said, 'Are you training yourself in zazen? Are you striving to become a sitting Buddha? If you are training yourself in zazen, I must tell you that the substance of zazen is neither sitting nor lying. If you're training yourself to become a sitting Buddha, I must tell you that the Buddha has no one form such as sitting. The Way, which has no fixed abode, allows of no distinctions. If you try to become a sitting Buddha, this is no less than killing the Buddha. If you cling to the sitting form you will not attain the essential truth.' Upon hearing this, Baso felt as refreshed as though he had had the most delicious of drinks.

P. KAPLEAU, *The Three Pillars of Zen*

DURING MEDITATION, we can focus all our attention on one object, and concentration can arise. This meditation is not passive or dull; in fact we must be very alert. We maintain concentration on the object, in the same way as the sun continues to shine on vegetation. We can also synchronise our breathing with out attention to the object, and this may improve our concentration. If we use a leaf as the object of concentration, we can see, through the leaf, the perfect oneness of mind and universe. Meditating on interbeing and interpenetration of reality is a means to destroy concepts, and using such means, we can arrive at a direct experience of ultimate reality in mind and body simultaneously.

THICH NHAT HANH, *The Sun Is My Heart*

SOMETIMES PEOPLE say that without a teacher, meditation can cause confusion and imbalance, but it is not always possible to find a highly developed teacher. People like that are rare, although it is usually possible to find teachers who have not yet fully realised the Way. If you are not able to study with a realised teacher, the most intelligent way to practice is to rely on the teacher within yourself.

THICH NHAT HANH, *The Sun Is My Heart*

YOU DO not feel feelings, think thoughts, or sensations any more than you hear hearing, see sight, or smell smelling. 'I feel fine' means that a fine feeling is present. It does not mean that there is one thing called 'I' and a separate thing called a feeling, so that when you bring them together this 'I' feels the fine feeling. There are no feelings but present feelings and whatever feeling is present is 'I'. No one ever found an 'I' apart from some present experience, or some experience apart from an 'I' – which is only to say that the two are the same thing.

ALAN WATTS in *Mystics and Sages*, Anne Bancroft

ONLY WHEN you have no thing in your mind and no mind in things are you vacant and spiritual, empty and marvelous.

TOKUSAN in *Zen Dictionary*, Ernest Wood

SEEING INTO nothingness – this is the true seeing, the eternal seeing.

SHEN-HUI in *On Having No Head*, D.E. Harding

PEOPLE ARE afraid to forget their [ordinary, dualistic] minds, fearing to fall through Emptiness with nothing to stay their fall. They do not know that Emptiness is not really empty, but the realm of the real Way.

JOHN BLOFELD, *The Zen Teaching of Huang Po*

OUR ORIGINAL nature is, in highest truth, void, silent, pure; it is glorious and mysterious peaceful joy – and that is all. Enter deeply into it by awakening to it yourself. That which is before you is it, in all its fullness, utterly complete.

JOHN BLOFELD, *The Zen Teaching of Huang Po*

BEFORE YOU begin meditation, move your body from right to left a few times, then take several slow, deep breaths. Hold your body erect, allowing your breathing to become normal again. Many thoughts will crowd into your mind … ignore them until they vanish. Do not allow the mind to become negative. Think that which you cannot think. In other words, think nothing. This is the proper way to meditate according to Zen teaching.

When you wish to stop, stand up slowly. Practice this meditation in the morning, in the evening, or at any leisure time. You will soon realise that your mental burdens are dropping away from you one by one, and that you are gaining a sort of intuitive power hitherto unnoticed. Do not think that the wise do not need to meditate. The wise and the dull should both take time for meditation. Constant practice will lead anyone to the realisation of truth.

NYOGEN SENZAKE, *Buddhism and Zen*

IN ZEN the three requirements are great faith, great doubt and great determination – these are the 'goods', and they are something that we *are,* not something that we *have.*

ERNEST WOOD, *Zen Dictionary*

SHUZAN HELD out his short staff and said, 'If you call this a short staff, you oppose its reality because you are attached to its name. If you do not call it a short staff, you ignore the fact of it. Now what do you want to call this?'

The comment: Shuzan wants to know what this is. It just is. Experience it. Don't talk about it.

G. KUBOSE, *Zen Koans*

ZAZEN DOES not mean ecstasy or the arousal of emotion or any particular condition of body and mind. It means returning, completely, to the pure, normal human condition. That condition is not something reserved for great masters and saints, there is nothing mysterious about it, it is within everyone's reach. Zazen means becoming intimate with oneself finding the exact taste of inner unity, and harmonising with universal life.

TAISEN DESHIMARU, *The Zen Way to the Martial Arts*

WHEN IN Zen there is the advice to give up all concepts, it must of course include the concept of no-concept.

ERNEST WOOD, *Zen Dictionary*

WHEN YOU rob a person of his pain and suffering, you rob him of his life, his freedom, his independence; you keep him dependent on you. This is a trap for therapists and healers and Zen teachers, too. After all, where would any of us be without our patients and students? But our practice is to get ourselves standing on our own two feet as quickly as possible and then to help others do the same. Ironically, it is the ones we most cherish whom we most often rob of their independence, because we tend to shield and overprotect them.

The more you talk and think about it,
the further astray you wander from the truth.

K. DURCKHEIM, *The Grace of Zen*

THROUGHOUT YOUR meditation, keep the sun of your awareness shining. Like the physical sun which lights every leaf and every blade of grass, our awareness lights our every thought and feeling, allowing us to recognise them, be aware of their birth, duration and dissolution, without judging or evaluating, welcoming or banishing them.

THICH NHAT HANH, *The Sun Is My Heart*

This is the last step of the journey. The boy is now mature and become a man. He is in the world again, and now he responds to people without effort for he is simple and free. His solitary quest is over and he is totally at home wherever he is.

WHEN WE look at a chair, we see the wood, but we fail to observe the tree, the forest, the carpenter, or our own mind. When we meditate on it, we can see the entire universe in all its inter-woven and interdependent relations in the chair. The presence of the wood reveals the presence of the tree. The presence of the leaf reveals the presence of the sun. The presence of the blossom reveals the presence of the apple. Meditators can see the one in the many and the many in the one. The chair is not separate. It exists only in its interdependent relations with everything else in the universe. It is because all other things are.

THICH NHAT HANH, *The Sun Is My Heart*

THE FIRST aim of sitting is to unify the mind. For the average person, whose mind is being pulled in many directions, sustained concentration is virtually impossible. Through the practice of zazen the mind becomes one-pointed so that it can be controlled. This process can be likened to utilising the sun's rays through a magnifying glass. When the rays of the sun are focused they become, of course, more intense. The human mind too functions more efficiently when it is concentrated and unified. Whether your desire is to see into your Self-nature or not, you can appreciate the effect on your well-being of mind integration.

MASTER YASUTANI in *The Three Pillars of Zen*, P. Kapleau

THIS PURE Mind, the source of everything, shines forever and on all with the brilliance of its own perfection. But the people of the world do not awake to it, regarding only that which sees, hears, feels and knows as mind. Blinded by their own sight, hearing, feeling and knowing, they do not perceive the spiritual brilliance of the source-substance. If they would only eliminate all conceptual thought in a flash, that source-substance would manifest itself like the sun ascending through the void and illuminating the whole universe without hindrance or bounds. Therefore, if you students of the Way seek to progress through seeing, hearing, feeling and knowing, when you are deprived of your perceptions, your way to Mind will be cut off and you will find nowhere to enter. Only realise that, though real Mind is expressed in these perceptions, it neither forms part of them nor is separate from them. You should not start reasoning from these perceptions, nor allow them to give rise to conceptual thought; yet nor should you seek the One Mind apart from them or abandon them in your pursuit of the Way. Do not keep them nor abandon them nor dwell in them nor cleave to them. Above, below and around you, all is spontaneously existing, for there is nowhere which is outside the Mind.

JOHN BLOFELD, *The Zen Teaching of Huang Po*

THE STRUGGLE between for and against is the mind's worst disease.

ERNEST WOOD, *Zen Dictionary*

ALL THE Buddhas and all sentient beings are nothing but the One Mind, beside which nothing exists. This mind, which is without beginning, is unborn and indestructible. It is not green nor yellow, and has neither form nor appearance. It does not belong to the categories of things which exist or do not exist, nor can it be thought of in terms of new or old. It is neither long nor short, big nor small, for it transcends all limits, measures, names, traces and comparisons. It is that which you see before you – begin to reason about it and you at once fall into error.

JOHN BLOFELD, *The Zen Teaching of Huang Po*

WHEN YOU are attached to form you must stop your wandering, look penetratingly into your inherent nature, and concentrating your spiritual energy, sit in zazen and break through.

BASSUI in *Crazy Clouds*, Perle Besserman

THERE IS a reality even prior to heaven and earth;
Indeed, it has no form, much less a name;
Eyes fail to see it;
It has no voice for ears to detect;
To call it Mind or Buddha violates its nature,
For it then becomes like a visionary flower in the air;
It is not Mind, nor Buddha;
Absolutely quiet, and yet illuminating in a mysterious
    way,
It allows itself to be perceived only by the clear-eyed.
It is truly beyond form and sound;
It is the Way, having nothing to do with words.
Wishing to entice the blind,
The Buddha has playfully let words escape his golden
    mouth;
Heaven and earth are ever since filled with entangling
    briars.
O my good friends gathered here,
If you desire to listen to the thunderous voice of the
    Way,
Exhaust your words, empty your thoughts,
For then you may come to recognise this One Essence.

DAI-O KOKUSHI in *Manual of Zen Buddhism*, D.T. Suzuki

THE ART OF ZEN

A HAIKU IS not a poem; it is not literature; it is a hand beckoning, a door half-opened, a mirror wiped clean. It is a way of returning to nature.

ERNEST WOOD, *Zen Dictionary*

M ODERN PAINTERS apply their mind only to brush and ink, whereas the ancients paid attention to the absence of brush and ink. If one is able to realise how the ancients applied their mind to the absence of brush and ink, one is not far from reaching the divine quality of painting.

TOSHIHIKO IZUTSU, *Toward a Philosophy of Zen Buddhism*

T HE ZEN of seeing is a way from half-sleep to full awakening. Suddenly there is the miracle of being really alive with all the senses functioning. The eye that sees is the I experiencing itself in what it sees. It becomes self-aware, it realises that it is an integral part of the great continuum of all that is. It sees things such as they are.

No thing is a mere symbol of anything but itself. A rose is not a symbol of love, nor a rock of strength. A rose is a rose experienced in its suchness. To draw it is to say 'Yes' to its and my existence.

FREDERICK FRANCK, *The Zen of Seeing*

THE PURPOSE of Zen philosophy and art is not to provide a reproduction of life in words or in paint, for the real thing is better than any reproduction. Their purpose is to give one the hint to see for oneself. Hence the Chinese artists understood better than any others the value of empty spaces, and in a certain sense what they left out was more important than what they put in; it was a tantalising reticence, a vacuum which drew out curiosity; they lifted just a corner of the veil to excite people to find out for themselves what lay beyond. This was the Taoist principle of *wu-wei,* of arriving at action through non-action. With a few strokes of the brush the Sung artist could achieve more than others could achieve after weeks of painstaking labour, for his strength was in his economy of force.

ALAN WATTS, *Does It Matter?*

MASTER SESSAN said: 'The secret of seeing things as they are is to take off our coloured spectacles. That being-as-it-is, with nothing extraordinary about it, nothing wonderful, is the great wonder. The ability to see things normally is no small thing; to be really normal is unusual. In that normality inspiration begins to bubble up.'

D.T. SUZUKI, *Essays in Zen Buddhism*

SOLITARY AUTUMN flower is seen quietly blooming against a white background. It is not a mere picture of a single flower, for the depicted flower conjures up the presence of Nature infinitely extending beyond it. And by so doing, the flower discloses to our inner eye the cosmic solitude and quietude of all solitary existents in the world. Even a fruit or vegetable can in this sense constitute the subject of a landscape painting. The most celebrated picture of 'Six persimmons' by Mu Ch'i is a good example. In its extreme simplification of the form of persimmons drawn in various tones of black ink, it is a pictorial representation of the vast cosmos. The underlying philosophy is Zen metaphysics which sees in one thing, in every single thing, all other things contained.

TOSHIHIKO IZUTSU, *Toward a Philosophy of Zen Buddhism*

THE GREAT mistake in swordsmanship is to anticipate the outcome of the engagement; you ought not to be thinking of whether it ends in victory or in defeat. Just let the Nature take its course, and your sword will strike at the right moment.'

D.T. SUZUKI, *Zen and Japanese Culture*

WHEN ONE goes to Obaku temple in Kyoto one sees carved over the gate the words 'The First Principle'. The letters are unusually large, and those who appreciate calligraphy always admire them as being a masterpiece. They were drawn by Kosen two hundred years ago.

When the master drew them he did so on paper, from which workmen made the larger carving in wood. As Kosen sketched the letters a bold pupil was with him who had made several gallons of ink for the calligraphy and who never failed to criticise his master's work.

'That is not good,' he told Kosen after the first effort.

'How is that one?'

'Poor. Worse than before,' pronounced the pupil.

Kosen patiently wrote one sheet after another until eighty-four First Principles had accumulated, still without the approval of the pupil.

Then, when the young man stepped outside for a few moments, Kosen thought: 'Now is my chance to escape his keen eye,' and he wrote hurriedly, with a mind free from distraction: 'The First Principle.'

'A masterpiece,' pronounced the pupil.

TREVOR LEGGETT, *The Old Zen Master*

HOW I would like people
To hear the sound of the snow falling
Through the deepening night.

ANNE BANCROFT, *The Luminous Vision*

ZAZEN, OR sitting meditation, is generally considered an indispensable preparation towards the Zen experience of satori [illumination]. It is a discipline of pointed mindfulness, persevered in to the point where the in-sight breaks through ... But I for one am not good at sitting still for long in one position. I believe that in Seeing/Drawing there is a way of awakening the 'Third Eye', of focusing attention until it turns into contemplation, and from there to the inexpressible fullness, where the split between the seer and what is seen is obliterated. Eye, heart, hand become one with what is seen and drawn, things are seen as they are – in their 'isness'. Seeing things thus, I know who I am!

It is in order to really SEE, to SEE ever deeper, ever more intensely, hence to be fully awake and alive, that I draw what the Chinese call the 'Ten Thousand Things' around me. Drawing is the discipline by which I constantly rediscover the world.

FREDERICK FRANCK, *The Zen of Seeing*

ORDER AND serendipity: these are the characteristics of the Zen garden, and they symbolise many things. Thus in the temple of Ryonanji there is a garden, or perhaps better just a space, mainly raked sand white with the faint lines of the rake worked around it. And rising through the sand are fifteen assorted rocks in five clumps. It is a mysterious geological poem; it is a kind of contemplative rock-sound. What does it mean? Any way of telling would fall foul of the Zen destruction of concepts, but for want of silence it is worth commenting that it echoes so much of Zen art – the blanks in the pictures are so many signs of the Void and of that true emptiness of mind which is the fullness of enlightenment. The raked sand is blank; the rocks are whatever may be dredged up, perhaps, in the sea of emptiness and they too are empty.

NINIAN SMART, *Background to the Long Search*

TREES SHOW the bodily form of the wind;
Waves give vital energy to the moon
To put it less poetically – human experience is determined as much by the nature of the mind and the structure of its senses as by the external objects whose presence the mind reveals.

ALAN WATTS in *The Spiritual Journey, Anne Bancroft*

FOR THE ZEN painter everything is inspirited ... The painter concentrates first and foremost on penetrating into the 'spirit' of the thing he wants to paint. The 'spirit' of a thing is the ... innermost ground of its being, lying beyond its external colour and form. It is this inscrutable spiritual force, the life-breath, the deepest essence of the thing, that is considered to make a painting a real piece of art, when the inspired painter has succeeded in transmitting it through brush and ink.

TOSHIHIKO IZUTSU, *Toward a Philosophy of Zen Buddhism*

IMMEDIATENESS OF action on your part will inevitably end in the [fencing] opponent's self-defeat. It is like a boat smoothly gliding down the rapids; in Zen, and in fencing as well, a mind of no-hesitation, no-interruption, no-mediacy, is highly valued. So much reference is made in Zen to a flash of lightning or to sparks issuing from the impact of two flint-stones. If this is understood in the sense of quickness, a grievous mistake is committed. The idea is to show immediateness of action, an uninterrupted movement of life-energy.

TAKUAN in *Spiritual Journey*, Anne Bancroft

A SOLDIER NAMED Nobushige came to Hakuin, and asked: 'Is there really a paradise and a hell?'

'Who are you?' inquired Hakuin.

'I am a samurai,' the warrior replied.

'You, a soldier!' exclaimed Hakuin. 'What kind of ruler would have you as his guard? Your face looks like that of a beggar.'

Nobushige became so angry that he began to draw his sword, but Hakuin continued: 'So you have a sword! Your weapon is probably much too dull to cut off my head.'

As Nobushige drew his sword Hakuin remarked: 'Here open the gates of hell!'

At these words the samurai, perceiving the master's discipline, sheathed his sword and bowed.

'Here open the gates of paradise,' said Hakuin.

PAUL REPS, *Zen Flesh, Zen Bones*

THE ROLE of Zen in the martial arts defies easy definition because Zen has no theory; it is an inner knowing for which there is no clearly stated dogma. Its ultimate aim is to free the individual from anger, illusion, and false passion.

JOE HYAM, *Zen in the Martial Arts*

THE MIND must always be in the state of 'flowing,' for when it stops anywhere that means the flow is interrupted and it is this interruption that is injurious to the well-being of the mind. In the case of the swordsman, it means death.

When the swordsman stands against his opponent, he is not to think of the opponent, nor of himself, nor of his enemy's sword movements. He just stands there with his sword which, forgetful of all technique, is ready only to follow the dictates of the unconscious. The man has effaced himself as the wielder of the sword. When he strikes, it is not the man but the sword in the hand of the unconscious that strikes.

JOE HYAM, *Zen in the Martial Arts*

ABOUT THE koan, you should single out the point where you have been in doubt all your life and put it upon your forehead. Is it a holy point or a commonplace one? Is it an entity or a non-entity? Press your question to its very end. Do not be afraid of plunging yourself into a vacuity; find out what it is that cherishes the sense of fear. Is it a void, or is it not?

TAI-HUI in *Studies in Zen*, D.T. Suzuki

WHAT MAKES swordsmanship come closer to Zen than any other art that has developed in Japan is that it involves the problem of death in the most immediately threatening manner. If the man makes one false movement he is doomed forever, and he has no time for conceptualisation or calculated acts. Everything he does must come right out of his inner mechanism, which is not under the control of consciousness. He must act instinctually and not intellectually. At the moment of the most intensely concentrated struggle for life and death, what counts most is time, and this must be utilised in the most effective way. If there were the slightest moment of relaxation the enemy would feel it instantly and lose no time in making use of it, which means your annihilation. It is not a matter of mere defeat and humiliation.

The moment of intense concentration is the moment when a perfect identification takes place between subject and object, the person and his behaviour. When this is not reached, it means that the field of consciousness has not yet been completely cleared up: that there still remains 'a subtle trace of thought' which interferes with an act directly and straight-forwardly issuing from the person – that is, psychologically speaking, from the Unconscious. The result is surely calamitous, for the threatening sword will strike the interfering gap of consciousness.

This is the reason why the swordsman is always advised to be free from the thought of death or from anxiety about the outcome of the combat. As long as there is any 'thought,' of whatever nature, that will most assuredly prove disastrous.

D.T. Suzuki, *Zen Doctrine of No Mind*

A GOOD MARTIAL artist puts his mind on one thing at a time. He takes each thing as it comes, finishes with it, and passes on to the next. Like a Zen master, he is not concerned with the past or the future, only with what he is doing at that moment. Because his mind is tight, he is calm and able to maintain strength in reserve. And then there will be room for only one thought, which will fill his entire being as water fills a pitcher.

Joe Hyam, *Zen in the Martial Arts*

IN THE landscape of spring there is neither high nor low;
The flowering branches grow naturally, some long, some short

R.H. Blyth, *Zen in English Literature*

The Art of Zen ↭ 105

WE MASTER archers say: with the upper end of the bow the archer pierces the sky, on the lower end, as though attached by a thread, hangs the earth. If the shot is loosed with a jerk there is a danger of the thread snapping. For purposeful and violent people the rift becomes final, and they are left in the awful centre between heaven and earth.

'What must I do, then?' I asked thoughtfully.

'You must learn to wait properly.'

'And how does one learn that?'

'By letting go of yourself, leaving yourself and everything of yours behind you so decisively that nothing more is left of you but a purposeless tension.'

EUGEN HERRIGEL, *Zen in the Art of Archery*

HAIKU IS a way of returning to nature, to our moon-nature, our cherry-blossom nature, in short to our true nature. It's a way in which the cold winter rain, the swallows of evening, even the very day in its hotness and the length of the night become truly alive, share in our humanity, speak their own silent and expressive language.

R.H. BLYTH in *The Spiritual Journey*, Anne Bancroft

THE MORNING glory which blooms for an hour
Differs not at heart from the giant pine,
Which lives for a thousand years.

R.H. BLYTH, *Zen in English Literature*

THE SUNG masters were pre-eminently landscape painters, creators of a tradition of 'nature painting' which has hardly been surpassed anywhere in the world. For it shows us the life of nature – of mountains, waters, mists, rocks, trees, and birds – as felt by Taoism and Zen. It is a world to which man belongs but which he does not dominate; it is sufficient to itself for it was not 'made for' anyone and has no purpose of its own. As Hsuan-chueh said:

Over the river, the shining moon; in the pine trees,
sighing wind;
All night long so tranquil – why? And for whom?

ALAN WATTS, in *The Spiritual Journey*, Anne Bancroft

THE WILD geese do not intend to cast their reflection;
The water has no mind to receive their image.

HAKUIN in *Zen in English Literature*, R.H. Blyth

The Art of Zen ✤ 107

EVEN WHEN the Zen monk or artist draws a solitary circle – one of the most common themes of *zenga* – it is not only slightly eccentric and out of shape, but the very texture of the line is full of life and verve, with the incidental splashes and gaps of the 'rough brush'. For the abstract or 'perfect' circle becomes concrete and natural – a living circle – and, in the same way, rocks and trees, clouds and waters appear to the Chinese eye as most like themselves when most unlike the intelligible forms of the geometer and architect.

ALAN WATTS, *The Way of Zen*

THUS THE aimless life is the constant theme of Zen art of every kind, expressing the artist's own inner state of going nowhere in a timeless moment. All men have these moments occasionally, and it is just then that they catch those vivid glimpses of the world which cast such a glow over the intervening wastes of memory – the smell of burning leaves on a morning of autumn haze, a flight of sunlit pigeons against a thundercloud, the sound of an unseen waterfall at dusk, or the single cry of some unidentified bird in the depths of a forest. In the art of Zen every landscape, every sketch of bamboo in the wind or of lonely rocks, is an echo of such moments.

ALAN WATTS in *The Spiritual Journey,* Anne Bancroft

SLEET FALLING;
Fathomless, infinite
Loneliness

>BASHO in *The Way of Zen*, Alan Watts

IN THE dark forest
A berry drops
The sound of water

>R.H. BLYTH, *Zen in English Literature*

THE STARS on the pond
Again the winter shower
Ruffles the water

>R.H. BLYTH, *Zen in English Literature*

ON A withered branch
The crow is perched
In the autumn evening

>R.H. BLYTH, *Zen in English Literature*

WITH THE evening breeze
The water laps
Against the heron's legs

R.H. BLYTH, *Zen in English Literature*

WHEN, JUST as they are,
White dewdrops gather
On scarlet maple leaves,
Regard the scarlet beads!

L. STRYCK, *Zen: Poems, Prayers, Sermons, Anecdotes,*
Interviews

BY ARRANGING several trees, bamboos and stones, a capable
Zen gardener can make people feel as if they were in deep
mountains and dark valleys while they only stand in a
small garden in the midst of a large town.

SOHAKU OGATA, *Zen for the West*

I ASK WHETHER Zen can be used by artists, as it might have been by the great master painter Sesshu, to achieve the proper state of mind for serious artistic production. The master's answer: 'Zen is not something to be "used." Zen art is nothing more than an expression of Zen spirit.'

L. STRYCK, *Zen: Poems, Prayers, Sermons*

THE ULTIMATE intent of the koan is to go beyond the limits of the intellect. What could not be solved by logic is then transferred to the deeper recesses of the mind. The koan refuses to be solved under easy conditions. But once solved, the koan is like a piece of brick used to knock at a gate; when the gate is opened the brick is thrown away. The koan is useful as long as the psychological doors are closed, but when they are opened, it may be forgotten. What one sees after the opening will be something quite unexpected, something that has never before even entered into one's imagination. But when the koan is re-examined from this newly acquired point of view, how marvellously suggestive, how fittingly constructed, although there is nothing artificial here!

D.T. SUZUKI, *Manual of Zen Buddhism*

ONCE A monk asked Joshu, 'Tell me what is the ultimate truth of Zen Buddhism?'

Joshu replied, 'The cypress tree in the courtyard.'

The whole world is the Cypress Tree. Joshu is the Cypress Tree. There is in short nothing other than the Awareness of the Cypress Tree, because at this metaphysical zero-point, Being itself in its very non-differentiation is illuminating itself as the Cypress Tree, unique and universal at the same time.

LU K'UAN YU, *Ch'an and Zen Teaching, Series 2*

THE QUESTION clear, the answer deep,
Each particle, each instant a reality,
A bird call shrills through mountain dawn:
Look where the old master sits, a rock, in Zen.

SONO in Zen: *Poems, Prayers, Sermons, Anecdotes, Interviews,*
L. Stryck

OUR TECHNIQUE has to be given up. We think, 'What!?' In judo, when the teacher tells us, 'You've mastered that. Now give it up for at least six months,' we think, 'What? I'm not allowed to do that? I go on the mat and I'm not allowed to use my big throw. I've got to try other things that I can't do – I get countered, I look an absolute fool!' Now many of us fail that test. We think, 'Oh no, no! I'm not going to do this,' and we go back to what we can do, and we get some successes. But those who've got faith in the teacher and who realise that the teacher's got faith in them, they persist and then they begin to develop a free movement, not fixed on one point – they can move freely. If the opportunity's here, they can take it; if it's there, they can take it – they're not fixed.

TREVOR LEGGETT, *Fingers and Moons*

REFRESHING, THE wind against the waterfall
As the moon hangs, a lantern, on the peak
And the bamboo window glows. In old age mountains
Are more beautiful than ever. My resolve:
That these bones be purified by rocks.

JAKUSEITSU in *Zen: Poems, Prayers, Sermons, Anecdotes,
Interviews*, L. Stryck

NOT A mote in the light above,
Soul itself cannot offer such a view.
Though dawn's not come, the cock is calling:
The phoenix, flower in beak, welcomes spring.

TSUGEN in *Zen: Poems, Prayers, Sermons, Anecdotes,*
Interviews, L. Stryck

ALWAYS ZEN is to be found, if at all, in immediate experience, the
firefly rather than the star.

L. STRYCK, *Zen: Poems, Prayers, Sermons*

THE BAMBOO shadows are sweeping the stairs,
But no dust is stirred;
Moonlight penetrates into the depth of the pool
But no trace is left in the water.

ERNEST WOOD, *Zen Dictionary*

THE AIM of every koan is to liberate the mind from the snare of language, which acts as a straitjacket to experience. Koans are so phrased that they deliberately throw sand into our eyes to force us to open our Mind's eye and see the world and everything in it without distortion. Koans take as their subjects tangible, down to earth objects such as a dog, a tree, a face, a finger to make us see, on the one hand, that each object has absolute value and, on the other, to arrest the tendency of the intellect to anchor itself in abstract concepts. But the import of every koan is the same: that the world is one interdependent Whole and that each separate one of us is that Whole.

MASTER YASUTANI in *The Three Pillars of Zen*, P. Kapleau

LIVING A ZEN LIFE

To TREAD the bird's path is an expression in Zen resembling 'living on the wing', instead of with attachment or clinging to particular objects. The idea is to live without a track, like a bird flying in the air, but this must not be mistaken for a goal, as it is only a way of release from a particular form of bondage, and will itself be transcended.

ERNEST WOOD, *Zen Dictionary*

In ZEN one would say: the completely enlightened being no longer rests on any external moral code, but naturally does good and refrains from doing evil, out of the very depth of the Heart.

D.T. SUZUKI, *Essays in Zen Buddhism*

IF YOU don't believe, just look at September, look at October!
The yellow leaves falling, falling, to fill both mountain and river.

BASHO in *The Spiritual Journey*, Anne Bancroft

WEALTHY DONORS invited Master Ikkyu to a banquet. The Master arrived there dressed in beggar's robes. His host, not recognising him in this garb, hustled him away: 'We cannot have you here at the doorstep. We are expecting the famous Master Ikkyu any moment.' The Master went home, there changed into his ceremonial robe of purple brocade, and again presented himself at his host's doorstep. He was received with due respect, and ushered into the banquet room. There, he put his stiff robe on the cushion he was to sit on, saying, 'I expect you invited the robe since you showed me away a little while ago,' and then left.

TREVOR LEGGETT, *A First Zen Reader*

THIS 'NON-STOPPING' mind is known as fluidity, which is also known as the 'empty mind' or 'everyday mind'. To have something in mind means that it is preoccupied and has no time for anything else. But to attempt to remove the thought already in it is to refill it with another something. So what to do! Do nothing! Don't solve it – dissolve it – not fuss, no fuss – it's the everyday mind, nothing special at all.

BRUCE LEE, *Striking Thoughts*

NEVER HAS it been more urgent to speak of seeing. Ever more gadgets, from cameras to computers, from art books to videotapes, conspire to take over our thinking, our feeling, our experiencing, our seeing. Onlookers we are, spectators …'Subjects' we are, that look at 'objects'. Quickly we stick labels on all that is, labels that stick once and for all. By these labels we recognise everything but no longer see anything. We know the labels on the bottles, but never taste the wine. Millions of people, unseeing, joyless, bluster through life in their halfsleep, hitting, kicking, and killing what they have barely perceived. They have never learned to see, or they have forgotten that man has eyes to see, to experience.

FREDERICK FRANCK, *The Zen of Seeing*

WHEN YOU'RE both alive and dead,
Thoroughly dead to yourself,
How superb
The smallest pleasure!

BUNAN in *One Robe, One Bowl*, John Stevens

AN OLD Master said: 'Turn your heart around and enter the origin. Do not search for what has sprung out of it! If you want to know the origin, then penetrate your own original heart. This heart is the source of all beings in the world and outside the world. When the heart stirs, various things arise. 'But when the heart itself becomes completely empty the various things also become empty. If your heart is driven round neither by good nor bad, then all things are just as they are.'

IRMGARD SCHLOEGL, *The Wisdom of the Zen Masters*

WHEN RYONEN was about to pass from this world, she wrote another poem:

Sixty-six times have these eyes beheld the changing
    scene of autumn,
I have had enough about moonlight,
Ask no more,
Only listen to the voice of pines and cedars when no wind
    stirs.

R.H. BLYTH, *Zen in English Literature*

HOW WONDROUSLY supernatural,
And how miraculous this!
I draw water, and I carry fuel.

D.T. SUZUKI, *Studies in Zen*

JUST BEFORE Ninakawa passed away the Zen master Ikkyu visited him. 'Shall I lead you on?' Ikkyu asked.

Ninakawa replied: 'I came here alone and I go alone. What help could you be to me?'

Ikkyu answered: 'If you think you really come and go, that is your delusion. Let me show you the path on which there is no coming and no going.'

With his words, Ikkyu had revealed the path so clearly that Ninakawa smiled and passed away.

PAUL REPS, *Zen Flesh, Zen Bones*

THE WOODPECKER
Keeps on in the same place:
Day is closing.

R.H. BLYTH, *Zen in English Literature*

LAYMAN P'ANG was once lying on his couch reading a sutra. A monk saw him and said: 'Layman! You must maintain dignity when reading a sutra.'
The Layman raised up one leg.
The monk had nothing to say.

TREVOR LEGGETT, *The Old Zen Master*

MIRACULOUS POWER and marvellous activity
Drawing water and hewing wood

ZENRIN in *The Luminous Vision*, Anne Bancroft

WITHOUT LOOKING forward to tomorrow, every moment you must think only of this day and this hour. Because tomorrow is un-fixed and difficult to know, you must think of following the Buddhist way while you live today … You must concentrate on Zen practice without wasting time, thinking that there is only this day and this hour. After that it becomes truly easy. You must forget about the good and bad of your nature, the strength or weakness of your power.

R. MASANUGA, *The Standpoint of Dogen and His Treatise on Time*

THE TREE is stripped,
All colour, fragrance gone,
Yet already on the bough,
Uncaring spring!

L. STRYCK, *Zen: Poems, Prayers, Sermons*

ALL BEINGS are from the very beginning awakened;
It is like ice and water;
Apart from water no ice can exist.
Outside sentient beings, where do we seek
     enlightenment?
Not knowing how near Truth is,
People seek it far away …
They are like him who, in the midst of water,
Cries out in thirst so imploringly.

HAKUIN in *Spiritual Journey*, Anne Bancroft

ORDINARY PEOPLE feel they must have reason for doing
something, but to practice with a goal in mind makes it
impossible to get to the state of no-mind.

NYOGEN SENZAKE, *Buddhism and Zen*

THIS BEING satisfied or proud is, after all, nothing more than a continuation of the thoughts of our foolish self. However, in our zazen, it is precisely at the point where this small self, our foolish self is unsatisfied or completely bewildered that the immeasurable natural life beyond the thoughts of the small self is activated. It is precisely at the point where we become completely lost that life operates.

KOSHO UCHIYAMA ROSHI, *Approach to Zen*

ONCE, ON a day in late March when I was sweeping the garden, a feeling suddenly overcame me: am I myself and the world not together one? Can there be anything like a solitary ego at all? I am now sweeping the garden with a bamboo broom. The broom moves, making a sound and turning its eyes to the ground, as it were. This ground is nothing other than a part of the whole earth. Then I myself am united to the whole earth. The sound of the broom could not arise if I myself and the broom and the whole earth did not exist here. They are inseparably connected.

H. DUMOULIN, *Zen Enlightenment*

ON MOUNT Wu-t'ai the clouds are steaming rice;
Before the ancient Buddha hall, dogs piss at heaven.

TOYO EICHO in *The Way of Zen*, Alan Watts

AT ONE stroke I forgot all my knowledge!
There's no use for artificial discipline,
For, move as I will, I manifest the ancient Way.

WU-TENG HUI-YUAN in *The Way of Zen*, Alan Watts

SITTING QUIETLY, doing nothing,
Spring comes, and the grass grows by itself.

TOYO EICHO in *The Way of Zen*, Alan Watts

'OH, HERE is the entrance to reality as it really is' said a disciple in the monastery garden … 'All things in living motion and as if inviting my gaze. All things are in their place or they dwell securely in their place and appear to breathe. I was able to discover the existence of a world not entered by knowledge. The colour of a flower was incomparably resplendent. Leaving nothing behind.'

H. DUMOULIN, *Zen Enlightenment*

THE SKYLARK:
Its voice alone fell,
Leaving nothing behind

TOYO EICHO in *The Way of Zen*, Alan Watts

ALL OF us are apprenticed to the same teacher that the religious institutions originally worked with: reality. Reality-insight says get a sense of immediate politics and history, get control of your own time; master the twenty-four hours. Do it well, without self-pity. It is as hard to get the children herded into the car pool and down the road to the bus as it is to chant sutras in the Buddha-hall on a cold morning. One move is not better than the other, each can be quite boring, and they both have the virtuous quality of repetition. Repetition and ritual and their good results come in many forms. Changing the filter, wiping noses, going to meetings, picking up around the house, washing dishes, checking the dipstick – don't let yourself think these are distracting you from your more serious pursuits. Such a round of chores is not a set of difficulties we hope to escape from so that we may do our 'practice' which will put us on a 'path' – it is our path.

CLAUDE WHITMYER, *Mindfulness and Meaningful Work*

TO THINK that, because you are ill, you must wait to practice until you are cured betrays a lack of the mind that seeks the Way. Our bodies are made up of a combination of the four great elements; who is there that can escape illness? The men of old did not all have bones of metal. If you only have the determination, you can practice, forgetting all other things. When the body confronts something vital, it habitually forgets the trivial and the petty. Because Zen is the vital thing, determine to investigate it for your whole life and determine not to pass your days in vain.

REIHO MASUNAGA, *A Primer of Soto Zen*

DROPPED OFF! Dropped off! This state must be experienced by you all; it is like piling fruit into a basket without a bottom, it is like pouring water into a bowl with a hole in it.

DOGEN in *Zen Doctrines of No Mind*, D.T. Suzuki

TO LEARN the way of the Buddha is to learn about oneself. To learn about oneself is to forget oneself. To forget oneself is to be enlightened by everything in the world. To be enlightened by everything is to let fall one's own body-mind, and the body-mind of the 'other.'

DOGEN in *Ch'an and Zen Teaching, Series 1*, Lu K'uan Yu

IF SOMEONE asks you about the meaning of existence, answer him in terms of non-existence. If he asks about the worldly, speak of the saintly. If he asks of the saintly, speak of the worldly. In this way, the interdependence and mutual involvement of the two extremes will bring to light the significance of the Way.

HUINENG in *Zen Doctrines of No Mind*, D.T. Suzuki

OUR SKILLS and works are but tiny reflections of the wild world that is innately and loosely orderly. There is nothing like stepping away from the road and heading into a new part of the watershed. Not for the sake of newness, but for the sense of coming home to our whole terrain. 'Off the trail' is another name for the Way, and sauntering off the trail is the practice of the wild. That is also where – paradoxically – we do our best work. But we need paths and trails and will always be maintaining them. You first must be on the path before you can turn and walk into the wild.

CLAUDE WHITMYER, *Mindfulness and Meaningful Work*

JUST PUT thoughts to rest and don't seek outwardly anymore. When things come up, then give them your attention; just trust what is functional in you at present, and you have nothing to be concerned about.

SOKEI-AN SASAKI in *Zen Notes*

DO NOT be antagonistic to the world of the senses. For when you are not antagonistic to it, it turns out to be the same as complete awakening.

SENG-TS'AN in *The Gospel According to Zen*, Robert Sohl

HOW I have found fault with that poor ego! As if it were to be despised and annihilated at once. As if it were not an indispensable part of my life-process, that primeval narcissistic ruthlessness needed for growing up, for survival, that I share with ducklings and dogs. Zen does not bid me destroy ego, but to see into ego, into its relative reality ... Until in the end you see that ego does not have to be cast out but to know its place, until it is 'expanded to embrace all', as Suzuki says; until ego and egolessness live at peace together.

FREDERICK FRANK, *The Zen of Seeing*

I T IS difficult to get up at 6am to do zazen when I've been awakened four times in the night, and it's nearly impossible to summon the willpower to do at 10.30 pm when I fall into bed. So what kind of practice do I have? It would be very easy to give up, except that I have almost a life-or-death feeling about my practice. Without it, I am swept along by events, more or less keeping my nose above water, collecting bruises from unseen rocks. With it, I keep (in small steps) getting more able to meet the moment with a naked soul. The glimpses I get during zazen let me know that it is possible to see through the chaos. The example of my teacher reminds me that it is eminently worth doing. And the mistakes I make with my children, coupled with the world's need for centred, compassionate people with clear vision, remind me that I must keep on. So I don't give up, I do what I can. For some periods I am able to sit every day for 25 minutes; for some periods I sit once a week. Sometimes I feel my awareness is deepening, sometimes I feel I'm sliding back.

ANNE BANCROFT, *Spiritual Journey*

A DISILLUSIONED YOUNG man went to the abbot of a Zen monastery, asking him if there was any short way to awakening as he didn't think he could stick meditation for long and would easily be pulled back into the world again. 'Can you stick at anything for long?' asked the abbot, 'What have you concentrated on most in your life?' 'Nothing special. I'm rich and don't have to work. The thing that interests me most is chess.' The abbot called for a chess board and told his attendant he was to be the young man's opponent. Then he called for a sword. To his attendant, he said:

'You have vowed obedience to me and now I need it of you. You will play a game with this youth and if you lose I shall cut off your head. If you win, I shall cut off the head of this man. If chess is the only thing he has ever bothered about in this life, he deserves to lose his head.'

They began to play. The young man felt the sweat trickling down him as he played for his life. The chessboard became the whole world; he was entirely concentrated on it. As the game went on, he seized his chance to launch a strong attack. He was going to win. Then he looked at the attendant opposite him. He saw a face of intelligence and sincerity, worn by years of austerity and effort. He thought of his own worthless life and a wave of compassion came over him. He deliberately made a blunder and then another, leaving himself defenceless.

Suddenly the abbot upset the board. The two contestants sat stupefied. 'There is no winner and no loser,' said the abbot, 'and no head will fall.' He turned to the young man. 'Only two things are needed – complete concentration and compassion. Today you have learnt them both. Even completely concentrated on the game, you could feel compassion and sacrifice your life for it. Now stay here and pursue your training in this spirit and your awakening is certain.'

ROBERT SOHL, *The Gospel According to Zen*

ZEN FOLLOWERS believe in the possibility of attaining full enlightenment both here and now through determined efforts to rise beyond conceptual thought and to grasp that intuitive knowledge which is the central fact of enlightenment. Furthermore, they insist that the experience is both sudden and complete. While the striving may require years, the reward manifests itself in a flash. But to attain this reward, the practice of virtue and dispassion is insufficient. It is necessary to rise above such relative concepts as good and evil, sought and found, enlightened and unenlightened, and all the rest.

JOHN BLOFELD, *The Zen Teaching of Huang Po*

A MAN WAS once asked what he had in him, he looked so calm and contented. In turn he asked the questioner what he had in him, he looked so uneasy and disheartened. One who has nothing in him is always happy, but someone with many desires never gets out of his misery.

> He walked the blade of a sword; he stepped on the ice of a
>   frozen river;
> He entered the vacant house;
> His desire to steal ceased forever.
> He returned to his own home,
> Saw the beautiful rays of the morning sun,
> And watched the moon and stars intimately.
> He walked the streets with ease,
> Enjoying the gentle breeze.
> At last he opened his treasure house.
> Until that moment he never dreamed
> He had owned those treasures from the very beginning.

GENRO in *The Iron Flute*, N. Senzaki

A S AWAKENING strikes at the primary root of existence, its attainment generally marks a turning point in one's life. The attainment, however, must be thoroughgoing and clear-cut; a lukewarm awakening, if there is such a thing, is worse than no awakening. Here is an example:

When Tokusan gained an insight into the truth of Zen he immediately took out all his commentaries on the Diamond Sutra, once so valued and indispensable that he carried them with him wherever he went, and set fire to them. He exclaimed: 'However deep one's knowledge of philosophy, it is like a piece of hair flying in the vastness of space; however important one's experience in worldly things, it is like a drop of water thrown into an unfathomable abyss.'

D.T. SUZUKI, *Zen Doctrines of No Mind*

MOUNTAINS AND RIVERS

BEFORE I had studied Zen for thirty years, I saw mountains as mountains and rivers as rivers. When I arrived at a more intimate knowledge, I came to the point where I saw that mountains are not mountains, and rivers are not rivers, but now that I have got to the very substance I am at rest. For it's just that I see mountains once again as mountains, and rivers once again as rivers.

CH'ING-YUAN in *Zen Doctrine of No Mind*, D.T. Suzuki

SHUN ASKED Ch'eng, saying, 'Can one get the Way so as to have it for one's own?'

'Your very body,' replied Ch'eng, 'Is not your own. How should the Way be?'

'If my body,' said Shun, 'is not my own, pray whose is it?'

'It is the delegated image of the Way,' replied Ch'eng. 'Your life is not your own. It is the delegated harmony of the Way. Your individuality is not your own. It is the delegated adaptability of the Way … You move, but know not how. You are at rest, but know not why … These are the operations of the laws of the Way. How then should you get the Way so as to have it for your own?'

LU K'UAN YU, *Ch'an and Zen Teaching, Series 2*

BEFORE PRACTISING meditation, we see that mountains are mountains [as objects to be climbed and made use of]. When we start to practise, we see that mountains are no longer mountains ... When we look deeply into matter, we see that it is like a beehive moving at a very great speed. People usually think that forms are stable and real, but according to the Buddha and modern science, form is made only of empty space. It is composed of countless molecules which are, in turn, composed of countless atomic and subatomic particles, all of which are held together by electromagnetic and nuclear forces ... Physicists say that when they enter the world of atomic particles, they can see clearly that our conceptualised world is an illusion ... After practising for a while, we see that mountains are again mountains ... In the third stage the mountains reveal themselves freely, and we call this 'true being'. It is beyond being and non-being. The mountains are there in their wonderful presence, not as an illusion. The notion of emptiness in Zen is very deep. It goes beyond the illusory world of being and non-being, yes and no. It is called 'true emptiness'. True emptiness is not emptiness. True emptiness is true being.

THICH NHAT HAHN, *The Heart of Understanding*

Mountains and Rivers ↜ 143

I N THE T'ang period a teacher practised zazen in a tree. People called him Bird's Nest Roshi. The governor of the province, Po Chu-i, who was also a Zen poet, went to see him. He called up to him:

'You look insecure, Bird's Nest Roshi. But perhaps you can tell me what all the Buddhas have taught?'

Bird's Nest replied:

'Always do good.
Never do evil.
Cultivate your mind.
All the Buddhas have taught this.'

Po Chu-i said: 'Always do good, never do evil; and cultivate your mind – I knew this when I was three years old.'

'Oh, yes,' said Bird's Nest Roshi, 'a three-year-old child may know it; but even an eighty-year-old man cannot put it into practice.'

ANNE BANCROFT, *Spiritual Journey*

THE SEA darkens;
The voices of the wild ducks
Are faintly white.

TOYO EICHO in *The Way of Zen*, Alan Watts

ENLIGHTENMENT, WHEN it comes, will come in a flash. There can be no gradual, no partial, enlightenment. The highly trained and zealous adept may be said to have prepared himself for enlightenment, but by no means can he be regarded as partially enlightened – just as a drop of water may get hotter and hotter and then, suddenly, boil; at no stage is it partly boiling, and, until the very moment of boiling, no qualitative change has occurred. In effect, however, we may go through three stages – two of non-enlightenment and one of enlightenment. To the great majority of people, the moon is the moon and the trees are trees. The next stage (not really higher than the first) is to perceive that moon and trees are not at all what they seem to be, since 'all is the One Mind'. When this stage is achieved, we have the concept of a vast uniformity in which all distinctions are void; and, to some adepts, this concept may come as an actual perception, as 'real' to them as were the moon and the trees before. It is said that, when enlightenment really comes, the moon is again very much the moon and the trees exactly trees; but with a difference, for the enlightened man is capable of perceiving both unity and multiplicity without the least contradiction between them!

JOHN BLOFELD, *The Zen Teaching of Huang Po*

WE MAY be told that the truth of Zen is obvious, that it is standing before our eyes every moment of the day, but this does not take us very far. There seems to be nothing in putting on one's clothes, washing one's hands or eating one's food which would indicate the presence of enlightenment. Yet when a monk asked Master Nan-ch'ua, 'What is the Way?' he replied, 'Usual life is the Way.' The monk asked again, 'How can we accord with it?' Nan-ch'an answered, 'It you try to accord with it you will get away from it.' For life, even as the ordinary humdrum series of daily events, is something essentially ungraspable and indefinable; never for a moment does it stay the same; we can never make it stand still for analysis and definition … Therefore a Zen master when asked, 'What is the Way?' replied immediately, 'Walk on!' for we can only understand life by keeping pace with it and accepting its magic-like transformations and unending changes. By this acceptance the Zen follower is filled with a great sense of wonder, for everything is perpetually becoming new. The beginning of the universe is now, for all things are at this moment being created, and the end of the universe is now, for all things are at this moment passing away.

ALAN WATTS in *The Luminous Vision*, Anne Bancroft

A CONFUCIAN poet once came to Zen master Hui-t'ang to ask for the secret of his teaching. The master quoted one of the sayings of Confucius: 'Do you think I am hiding things from you? Indeed, I have nothing to hide from you.' Since Hui-t'ang would not allow any more questions, the poet went away deeply puzzled. But a short time after, the two went for a walk together in the mountains. As they were passing a bank of wild laurel the master turned to the poet and asked, 'Do you smell it?' 'Yes,' replied the poet. 'You see,' said the master, 'I have nothing to hide from you.' At once the poet was enlightened.

ANNE BANCROFT, *Spiritual Journey*

PO-CHANG had so many students that he had to open a second monastery. To find a suitable person as its master, he called his monks together and set a pitcher before them, saying:

'Without calling it a pitcher, tell me what it is.'

The head monk said, 'You couldn't call it a piece of wood.'

At this the monastery cook kicked the pitcher over and walked away. The cook was put in charge of the new monastery.

D.T. SUZUKI, *Studies in Zen*

I TOOK A walk. Suddenly I stood still, filled with the realisation that I had no body or mind. All I could see was one great illuminating Whole – omnipresent, perfect, lucid and serene. It was like an all-embracing mirror from which the mountains and rivers of the earth were projected ... I felt as clear and transparent as though my body and mind did not exist at all.

HAN SHAN in Spiritual Journey, Anne Bancroft

EARTH, MOUNTAINS, **rivers – hidden** in this nothingness.
In this nothingness – **earth, mountains,** rivers revealed.
Spring flowers, winter
There's no being nor non-being, nor denial itself

SAISHO in One Robe, One Bowl, John Stevens

A SPIRITUALITY OF delight is one in which we will often say, 'Ah!' A Zen master once said: 'Have you noticed how the pebbles of the road are polished and pure after the rain? And the flowers? No words can describe them. One can only murmur an "Ah!" of admiration. We should understand the "Ah!" of things.'

ANNE BANCROFT, Spiritual Journey

ONE DAY, while Nan-ch'uan was living in a little hut in the mountains, a strange monk visited him just as he was preparing to go to his work in the fields. Nan-ch'uan welcomed him, saying, 'Please make yourself at home. Cook anything you like for your lunch, then bring some of the left-over food to me along the road which leads to my work place.' Nan-ch'uan worked hard until evening and came home very hungry. The stranger had cooked and enjoyed a good meal by himself, then thrown away all the food and broken all the cooking pots. Nan-ch'uan found the monk sleeping peacefully in the empty hut, but when he rested his own tired body beside the stranger's, the latter got up and went away. Years later Nan-ch'uan told the story to his disciples with the comment, 'He was such a good monk, I miss him even now.' Zen takes food from a hungry man and the sword from a soldier. Anything to which one attaches oneself most is the real cause of suffering. The strange monk wished to give Nan-ch'uan nothing but true freedom. Later, when Nan-ch'uan told his disciples how he missed the old thief, he must have been enjoying his real freedom in everlasting gratitude to this unnamed teacher.

GENRO in *The Iron Flute*, Nyogen Senzaki

MOUNTAINS DO not lack the qualities of mountains. Therefore they always abide in ease and always walk. You should examine in detail this quality of the mountains walking.

Mountains' walking is just like human walking. Accordingly, do not doubt mountains' walking even though it does not look the same as human walking.

If you doubt mountains walking, you do not know your own walking; it is not that you do not walk, but that you do not know or understand your own walking.'

DOGEN in Impermanence Is Buddha-Nature, *Joan Stambaugh*

THE SINGLE aim of the true Zen follower is so to train his mind that all thought-processes based on the dualism inseparable from 'ordinary' life are transcended, their place being taken by that intuitive knowledge which, for the first time, reveals to a man what he really is. If all is one, then knowledge of a being's true self-nature – his original self – is equally a knowledge of all-nature, the nature of everything in the universe. Those who have actually achieved this tremendous experience, whether as Christians, Buddhists or members of other faiths, are agreed as to the impossibility of communicating it in words. They may employ words to point the way to others, but, until the latter have achieved the experience for themselves, they can have but the merest glimmer of the truth – a poor intellectual concept of something lying infinitely beyond the highest point ever reached by the human intellect.

JOHN BLOFELD, *The Zen Teaching of Huang Po*

SILENTLY AND serenely, one forgets all words,
Clearly and vividly, it appears before you.
When one realises it, time has no limits.
When experienced, your surroundings come to life.
Singularly illuminating is this bright awareness,
Full of wonder is the pure illumination.
The moon's appearance, a river of stars,

Snow-clad pines, clouds hovering on mountain peaks.
In darkness, they glow with brightness.
In shadows, they shine with a splendid light.
Like the dreaming of a crane flying in empty space,
Like the clear, still water of an autumn pool,
Endless aeons dissolve into nothingness,
Each indistinguishable from the other.

HUNG CHIH in *Buddhism and Zen*, Nyogen Senzake

AFTER ENTERING the world of elementary particles, scientists cannot find anything essential [substantial] in the world of matter. Meditators too realise that all phenomena interpenetrate and inter-are with all other phenomena, so in their everyday lives they look at a chair or an orange differently from most people. When they look at mountains and rivers, they see that 'rivers are no longer rivers and mountains are no longer mountains' … However, when they want to go for a swim they have to go into the river. When they return to everyday life, 'mountains are again mountains, rivers are again rivers.'

THICH NHAT HAHN, *The Diamond that Cuts through Illusion*

BLUE MOUNTAINS and green woods
Are our eminent teacher's clear face.
Do you understand this face?

SEUNG SAHN, *Bone of Space*

NOTHING WHATEVER is hidden;
From of old, all is clear as daylight.

The old pine-tree speaks divine wisdom;
The secret bird manifests eternal truth.

There is no place to seek the mind;
It is like the footprints of the birds in the sky.

The wild geese do not intend to cast their reflection;
The water has no mind to receive their image.
Scoop up the water and the moon is in your hands;
Hold the flowers and your clothes are scented with
them.
Mountains and rivers, the whole earth –
All manifest forth the essence of being.

The blue hills are of themselves blue hills;
The white clouds are of themselves white clouds.
In the landscape of spring there is neither high nor low;
The flowering branches grow naturally, some long, some
short.
We sleep with both legs outstretched,
Free of the true, free of the false.

For long years a bird in a cage,
Today, flying along with the clouds.

Verses from THE ZENRIN in *The Gospel According to Zen*,
Robert Sohl

OUR ORIGINAL Nature is, in highest truth, devoid of any atom of objectivity. It is void, omnipresent, silent, pure; it is glorious and mysterious peaceful joy – and that is all. Enter deeply into it by awakening to it yourself. That which is before you is it, in all its fullness, utterly complete. There is nothing beside. It is pure Being, which is the source of everything and which, whether appearing as sentient beings or as Buddhas, as the rivers and mountains of the world which has form, as that which is formless, or as penetrating the whole universe, is absolutely without distinctions, there being no such entities as self and others.

JOHN BLOFELD, *The Zen Teaching of Huang Po*

THE
COMPASSIONATE
TEACHER

THE BEST way to help the world is to be with our situation, exactly as it is. If we're completely willing to be what is, our vision can clear and we know better what to do. Each time we go into the suffering and let it be, our vision enlarges. Letting be is non-attachment, what practice is all about. It's like climbing a mountain. As we ascend, we see more and more. And the more we see – the clearer our vision – the more we know what to *do,* both personally and on the level of social action.

THICH NHAT HAHN, *The Diamond that Cuts through Illusion*

A MONK ASKED his teacher: 'What is my Self?'
    The teacher answered: 'There is something deeply hidden within yourself, and you must be acquainted with its hidden activity.'

The monk then asked to be told what this hidden activity was. The teacher just opened and closed his eyes.

It is the opening and closing of the eyes that is Zen. But this has to be pondered in the heart, as with all that is worthwhile it can only be revealed but not explained.

FREDERICK FRANCK, *The Zen of Seeing*

FOR THE study of Zen there are three essential requirements. The first is a great root of faith; the second is a great ball of doubt; the third is a great tenacity of purpose. One who lacks any of these is like a three-legged stool with one broken leg.

> MASTER HAKUIN in *Zen: Direct Pointing to Reality*, Anne Bancroft

THE KOAN I ordinarily give my pupils is: 'All things return to the One; where does the One return?' I make them search after this. To search after it means to awaken a great inquiring spirit for the ultimate meaning of the koan. The manyness of things returns to the One, but where does the One finally return? I say to them: Make this inquiry with all the strength that lies in your personality, giving yourself no time to relax in this effort. In whatever physical position you are, and in whatever business you are employed, never pass your time idly. Where does the One finally return? Try to press your spirit of inquiry forward, steadily and uninterruptedly. When your searching spirit comes to this stage, the time has come for your spiritual flower to burst out.

> KAO-FENG in *Studies in the Lankavatara Sutra*, D.T. Suzuki

VERY OFTEN I embrace people. Hug them. I warmly kiss them on the cheeks or give them a pat on the back. But I can also stand back, and say no, this is not the time. That's a very subtle matter about which we know as parents. Sometimes you're very firm with your child, and sometimes you're bestowing all the love and affection you can. But they know that love is there all the time, no matter how firm the discipline. So I hope what all of us are keeping in our hearts here is pure and warm practice, pure and warm mind. If you coldly remain apart from things, after all, that's not *it*.

MAURINE STUART in *Meetings with Remarkable Women*, Lenore Friedman

WHILE ZEN teaching consists in grasping the spirit by transcending form, it unfailingly reminds us of the fact that the world in which we live is a world of particular forms and that the spirit expresses itself only by means of form.

D.T. SUZUKI, *Zen Doctrines of No Mind*

THE STUDY of Zen is like drilling wood to get fire. The wisest course is to forge straight ahead without stopping. If you pause at the first sign of heat, and then again as soon as the first wisp of smoke arises, even though you go on drilling for years, you will never see a spark of fire. My native place is close to the seashore, barely a hundred paces from the beach. Suppose a man of my village is concerned because he does not know the flavour of sea water, and wants to go and taste it for himself. If he turns back after having taken only a few steps, or even if he retreats after having taken a hundred steps, in either case when will he ever know the ocean's bitter, salty taste? But, though a man comes from as far as the mountains of Koshu, if he goes straight ahead without stopping, within a few days he will reach the shore, and the moment he dips the tip of one finger into the sea and licks it, he will instantly know the taste of the waters of the distant oceans and the nearby seas, of the southern beaches and the northern shores, in fact of all the sea water in the world.

DOGEN in *Zen: Direct Pointing to Reality*, Anne Bancroft

THE ZEN way of teaching is to demonstrate Reality rather than talk about it, and is always to be taken seriously, although it is never solemn. To see it in its proper teaching capacity we have to overcome our tendency to put everything into words. Words are essential; but the snag is that when we rely too much on words we begin to substitute a world of indirect knowledge – knowledge *about* – for the immediate intense impact of what is actually there before thoughts and words arise. By using the right words for each situation, we can live our lives through without ever experiencing anything directly. The central methods of Zen are aimed at helping a pupil see that the conventional ways in which the world is conceptualised are useful for particular purposes but lack substance; when the concept-world is broken through, the pupil will come to the experience of unmediated Reality – the discovery of the ineffable wonder which is existence itself.

ANNE BANCROFT, *Zen: Direct Pointing to Reality*

SOMEONE ASKED Fenyang, 'What is the work of a teaching master?' Fenyang replied, 'Impersonally guiding those with affinity.'

ANNE BANCROFT, *The Luminous Vision*

The Compassionate Teacher ❦ 163

TANZAN AND Ekido were once travelling together down a muddy road. A heavy rain was still falling.

Coming around a bend, they met a lovely girl in a silk kimono and sash, unable to cross the intersection.

'Come on, girl,' said Tanzan at once. Lifting her in his arms, he carried her over the mud.

Ekido did not speak again until that night when they reached a lodging temple. Then he no longer could restrain himself. 'We monks don't go near females,' he told Tanzan, 'especially not young and lovely ones. It is dangerous. Why did you do that?'

'I left the girl there,' said Tanzan. 'Are you still carrying her?'

PAUL REPS, *Zen Flesh, Zen Bones*

WHEN ENLIGHTENED Zen masters set up teachings for a spiritual path, the only concern is to clarify the mind to arrive at its source. It is complete in everyone, yet people turn away from this basic mind because of their illusions.

SOKEI-AN SASAKI in *Zen Notes*

THE WORDS of buddhas and Zen masters are just tools, means of gaining access to truth. Once you are clearly enlightened and experience truth, all the teachings are within you.

Then you look upon the verbal teachings of buddhas and Zen masters as something in the realm of reflections or echoes, and you do not wear them around on your head.

SOKEI-AN SASAKI in *Zen Notes*

ZEN CANNOT be attained by lectures, discussions, and debates. Only those of great perceptive capacity can clearly understand it. For this reason the ancient adepts did not waste a moment. Even when they weren't calling on teachers to ascertain specific truths, they were involved in real Zen practice, so they eventually attained mature serenity in a natural way. They were not wrapped up in the illusions of the world.

SOKEI-AN SASAKI in *Zen Notes*

ZEN LIVING is a most direct shortcut, not requiring the exertion of the slightest bit of strength to attain enlightenment and master Zen right where you are.

But because Zen seekers are searching too eagerly, they think there must be a special principle, so they try to describe it to themselves mentally, in a subjective way.

Thus they are swept by the machinations of emotive and intellectual consciousness into something that is created and will perish.

They cling to this created, perishable law, rule, principle, or way of life, as something ultimate. This is a serious misstep.

This is why it is said, 'Do not talk about ultimate reality with your mind on what is created and destructible.'

SOKEI-AN SASAKI in *Zen Notes*

MASTER GANTO said to a brother: 'Whatever the great masters of Zen say, however they expound the teachings, of what use is all their learning and understanding to another person? That which gushes out from your own heart – that is what embraces heaven and earth.

D.T. SUZUKI, *Essays in Zen Buddhism*

KEN-O and his disciple Menzan were eating a melon together. Suddenly the master asked, 'Tell me, where does all this sweetness come from?'

'Why,' Menzan quickly swallowed and answered, 'it's a product of cause and effect.'

'Bah! That's cold logic!'

'Well,' Menzan said, 'from where then?'

'From that very "where" itself, that's where.'

L. STRYCK, *Zen: Poems, Prayers, Sermons*

IN YOUR physical body, what can you call Mind or Buddha? Now intensely ask yourself, 'What is this which can't be named or intellectually known?' If you profoundly question 'What is it that lifts the hands, moves the legs, speaks, hears?' your reasoning will come to a halt, every avenue being blocked, and you won't know which way to turn. But relentlessly continue your inquiry as to this subject. Abandon intellect and relinquish your hold on everything. When with your whole heart you long for liberation for its own sake, beyond every doubt you will become enlightened.

MASTER IGUCHI in *The Three Pillars of Zen*, P. Kapleau

RYOKAN, A Zen master, lived a simple kind of life in a little hut at the foot of a mountain. One evening a thief visited the hut, only to find there was nothing in it to steal.

Ryokan returned and caught him. 'You may have come a long way to visit me,' he told the prowler, 'and you should not return empty-handed. Please take my clothes as a gift.' The thief was bewildered. He took the clothes and ran away.

Ryokan sat naked, watching the moon. 'Poor fellow,' he mused, 'I wish I could give him this beautiful moon.'

The thief
Left it behind –
The moon at the window.

ROBERT SOHL, The Gospel According to Zen

THERE WAS once a monk, Hyakujo, who was walking with his master, Baso. Baso saw birds flying by and said, 'Where have they gone?' Hyakujo replied, 'They have flown away.' Baso grabbed Hyakujo's nose and twisted it really hard. Hyakujo shouted out, 'Ouch! What are you doing?' Baso wanted him to see the true situation! Where could the birds have gone? Is there any place to go? Any place to hide? Any place that is not home?

K. DURCKHEIM, The Grace of Zen

KYOGEN WENT to Master Yisan and asked him to teach him the essence of Zen. But Yisan replied: 'I really have nothing to impart to you. For whatever I can tell you is my own and can never be yours.' Disappointed, Kyogen decided to burn all his study notes and retire altogether from the world to spend the rest of his life in solitude and simplicity. He reasoned: 'What is the use of studying Zen, which is so difficult to understand and which is too subtle to receive as instruction from another? I will be a plain, homeless monk, troubled with no desire to master things too deep for thought.' He went away and built a hut in the countryside. One day he was sweeping the ground when a pebble which he had swept away struck a bamboo; the unexpected sound brought his mind to a state of awakening. His joy was boundless. He suddenly realised the kindness of Yisan in refusing him instruction, for now he saw that this experience could not have happened to him if Yisan had been unkind enough to explain things to him.

ROBERT SOHL, *The Gospel According to Zen*

ONLY ATTAIN the essential and never worry about the insignificant.

TREVOR LEGGETT, *The Old Zen Master*

A KOAN IS a problem given by a teacher to a student for solution. The student must solve it primarily alone, although a teacher will occasionally give some help. To work upon a koan, you must be eager to solve it; to solve a koan, you must face it without thinking of it. The more you pound it in cognition, the more difficult it will be to obtain a solution. Two hands brought together produce a sound. What is the sound of one hand? This is a koan. If you think that there is no such sound, you are mistaken.

A Zen koan is nothing but nonsense to outsiders, but for a student of Zen it is a gate to enlightenment. Intellectual gymnastics, no matter how superior or refined, could never solve a koan; in fact, a koan is given to force a student beyond intellection. Do not work upon more than one koan at a time, and do not discuss a koan with any person other than your teacher. Just face the question without thinking about anything else. Without neglecting everyday duties your every leisure moment should be spent exercising the mind with the koan.

NYOGEN SENZAKE, *Buddhism and Zen*

To SAY that once you are satisfied with what you are, you will grow no more, is a superficial understanding. Real growth begins when you get at the reality of what you are, when you can say 'It is absolutely all right,' even though it may be poor and miserable.

TREVOR LEGGETT, *The Old Zen Master*

BOUNDLESS AND free is the sky of transcendence,
Bright the full moon of wisdom!
Truly, is anything missing now?
Nirvana is right here, before our eyes;
This very place is the Lotus Land,
This very body, the Buddha.

HAKUIN in *Crazy Clouds*, Perle Besserman

IN ORIENTAL countries there have been many thousands of students who have practised Zen meditation and obtained its fruits. Do not doubt its possibilities because of the simplicity of its method. If you cannot find the truth within yourself, where else do you expect to find it?

NYOGEN SENZAKE, *Buddhism and Zen*

TO THE beloved company of the stars, the moon, and the
    sun;
to ocean, air, and the silence of space;
to jungle, glacier, and desert,
soft earth, clear water, and fire on my hearth.
To a certain waterfall in a high forest;
to night rain upon the roof and the wide leaves,
grass in the wind, tumult of sparrows in a bush,
and eyes which give light to the day.

LU K'UAN YU, *Ch'an and Zen Teaching, Series 1*

ALL THINGS being empty, so is the mind. As the mind is
empty, all is. My mind is not divisible: all is contained in
my every thought, which appears as enlightenment to the
wise, illusion to the stupid. Yet enlightenment and illusion are
one. Do away with both, but don't remain 'in between' either. In
this way you will be emptiness itself, which, stainless and devoid
of the interrelationship of things, transcends realization. In this
way the true Zen priest commonly conducts himself.

L. STRYCK, *Zen: Poems, Prayers, Sermons*

I T IS a paradox: when there is no fixed abode, no fixed home, every place is home. It works the same way with our minds. If the only place we feel at home is within our own prejudices and opinions and ideas, then our minds are fixated, stuck. Then we feel at home and friendly only with people who agree with our philosophy.

K. DURCKHEIM, *The Grace of Zen*

O NE DAY Banzan was walking through a market. He overheard a customer say to the butcher, 'Give me the best piece of meat you have.' 'Everything in my shop is the best,' replied the butcher. 'You can not find any piece of meat that is not the best.' At these words Banzan was enlightened. The comment: This is the core of Zen teaching. The rose is best as a rose. The lily is best as a lily. Each individual is the best in the world. One's only obligation is to bring out one's best.

G. KUBOSE, *Zen Koans*

EMPEROR: GUDO, what happens to the man of enlightenment and the man of illusion after death?
Gudo: How should I know, sir?
Emperor: Why, because you're a master!
Gudo: Yes, sir, but not a dead one!

L. STRYCK, *Zen: Poems, Prayers, Sermons*

RABBITS AND horses have horns:
Cows and sheep have none.

This statement does not aim to describe the ultimate reality of Zen, but to precipitate an awakening to it. The ordinary person, bound as he or she is by the strait-jacket of logic, exists in a world of half-truths: he sees that a rabbit is not a cow but does not see that, because of its mutual interpenetration with all things, it is also a cow. Thus, such a mad statement as above is a tool which a master employs to jolt his students into an immediate experience of Zen. In the mind of the pupil, the illogical half-truth is combined with the mundane half-truth that he takes for granted, and an insight into the whole truth of Zen results.

GREGORY NOYES, *Middle Way, Spring 1979*

ONE DAY a monk came to a master and asked him, 'I have been here under you for many years, and my coming to you was expressly to study Zen. But so far you have not imparted to me any Zen teaching. If this continues, I shall have to leave you, to my great regret.' The master replied, 'In the morning when you come and salute me with 'Good morning!' I salute you back, 'Good morning! How are you?' When you bring me a cup of tea I gratefully drink it. When you do anything else for me I acknowledge it. What other teachings do you want to have from me?' There is no special teaching – the most ordinary things in our daily life hide some deep meaning that is yet most plain and explicit; only our eyes need to see where there is a meaning. Unless this eye is opened there will be nothing to learn from Zen.

D.T. SUZUKI, *Middle Way*, May 1976

HUANG PO was asked: 'From all you have just said, Mind is the Buddha; but it is not clear as to what sort of mind is meant by this "Mind which is the Buddha." How many minds have you got?'

'But is the Buddha the ordinary mind or the Enlightened mind?'

'Where on earth do you keep your "ordinary mind" and your "Enlightened mind"?'

'In the teaching it is stated that there are both. Why does Your Reverence deny it?'

'In the teaching it is clearly explained that the ordinary and enlightened minds are illusions. You don't understand. All this clinging to the idea of things existing is to mistake vacuity for the truth. How can such conceptions not be illusory? Being illusory, they hide Mind from you. If you would only rid yourselves of the concepts of ordinary and Enlightened, you would find that there is no other Buddha than the Buddha in your own Mind.'

JOHN BLOFELD, *The Zen Teaching of Huang Po*

IF YOU want to realise your own Mind, you must first of all look into the source from which thoughts flow. Sleeping and working, standing and sitting, profoundly ask yourself, 'What is my own Mind?' with an intense yearning to resolve this question. This is called 'training' or 'practice' or 'desire for truth' or 'thirst for realisation.' What is termed zazen is no more than looking into one's own mind. It is better to search your own mind devotedly than to read and recite innumerable sutras every day.

MASTER BASSUI in *The Three Pillars of Zen*, P. Kapleau

THOUGH MANY may talk of The Way of the Buddhas as something to be reached by various pious practices and by study, you must have nothing to do with such ideas. A perception, sudden as blinking, that subject and object are one, will lead to a deeply mysterious wordless understanding; and by this understanding you will awaken to the truth of Zen. You must clearly understand that this Way is the Void which depends on nothing and is attached to nothing. It is all-pervading, spotless beauty; it is the self-existent and uncreated Absolute.

JOHN BLOFELD, *The Zen Teaching of Huang Po*

ZEN IN THE WEST

A JAPANESE ZEN master was asked recently to comment on Zen transmission to a new culture, as in its current transmission to the West. He raised one eyebrow and said, 'The first hundred years are the hardest.'

KENNETH KRAFT, *Zen Tradition and Transition*

I DON'T TEACH you to put on anything; I ask you to take off – to take the sawdust out of your mind.

M. FARKAS, *The Zen Eye*

IF YOU listen with your inner ear, your Zen Eye will open, and as your mind clears, your own wisdom will appear. From my standpoint, this New York civilisation is Buddhist; we do not need to do anything more than enjoy it. I live here and I enjoy it. We do not need to wipe out New York and go back to the mountains. What is wrong is that we do not recognise this life. Don't disdain life, live in it. Do not live in it as though you were in a dream. You have the treasure, the great jewel, in your hand. Open your hand and look at it.

M. FARKAS, *The Zen Eye*

As HUI Neng saw, it really makes no difference whatever if external objects are present in the 'mirror' of consciousness. There is no need to exclude or suppress them. Enlightenment does not consist in being without them. True emptiness ... is attained when the light of wisdom breaks through our empirical consciousness and floods with its intelligibility not only our whole being but all the things that we see and know around us. We are thus transformed in the wisdom light, we 'become' that light, which in fact we are.

THOMAS MERTON, *Mystics and Zen Masters*

YOUR ATTITUDE toward a saint will be the same as that toward a criminal. When you meet a saint, you will not smile, and when you meet a criminal, you will not frown. You will communicate with everyone as with yourself. You do not need to take any special attitude toward anyone you confront. This is the usual attitude of Zen students. Do not feel that you must maintain your dignity, or impress your greatness upon anyone. Meet everyone just as you would meet the soul of the universe.

M. FARKAS, *The Zen Eye*

THE REAL reason why human life can be so utterly exasperating and frustrating is not because there are facts called death, pain, fear, or hunger. The madness of the thing is that when such facts are present, we circle, buzz, writhe, and whirl, trying to get the 'I' out of the experience ... While the notion that I am separate from my experience remains, there is confusion and turmoil. Because of this, there is neither awareness nor understanding of experience, and thus no real possibility of assimilating it. To understand this moment I must not try to be divided from it; I must be aware of it with my whole being. This, like refraining from holding my breath for ten minutes, is not something I *should* do. In reality, it is the only thing I *can* do. Everything else is the insanity of attempting the impossible.

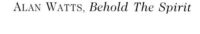

ALAN WATTS, *Behold The Spirit*

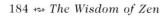

'THIS IS a tree.' Obviously *this* and *tree* are not actually the same thing. *Tree* is a word, a noise. It is not this experienced reality to which I am pointing. To be accurate, I should have said, 'This (pointing to the tree) is symbolised by the noise *tree.*'

If, then, the real tree is not the word or the idea *tree,* what is it? If I say that it is an impression on my senses, a vegetable structure, or a complex of electrons, I am merely putting sets of words and symbols in place of the original noise, *tree.* I have not said *what* it is at all. I have also raised other questions: 'What are my senses?' 'What is a structure?' 'What are electrons?' ... We can never say *what* these things are ... The word and idea *tree* has remained currency for many centuries, but real trees have behaved in a very odd way. I can try to describe their behaviour by saying that they have appeared and disappeared, that they been in a constant state of change, and that they flow in and out of their surroundings ... But this does not really say what they have done, because *disappear, change, flow,* and *surroundings* are still noises representing something utterly mysterious.

ALAN WATTS in *Mystics and Sages*, Anne Bancroft

ANOTHER EXERCISE that helps us raise doubt is the koan 'Who am I?' The question is designed to let you keep probing all the different concepts you have about yourself. Again, you make a list. You might start with your name: 'I'm Bernie.' Then again, 'I'm a father, or I'm a brother.' And so on. But whoever you come up with is not who you are. It's one of the roles you play. But if you keep going, past all these roles and identities, you might actually find yourself in a state of not knowing. That's the state of doubt we're talking about. It's breaking up this logjam of concepts, where we have so many ideas that nothing new is happening.

BERNARD GLASSMAN, *Instructions to the Cook*

THOSE WHO speak against killing, and who desire to spare the lives of all conscious beings, are right. It is good to protect even animals and insects. But what about those persons who kill time, what about those who destroy wealth, and those who murder the economy of their society? We should not overlook them. Again, what of the one who preaches without enlightenment? He is killing Zen.

GA-SAN in *The Perennial Philosophy*, A. Huxley

BIRTH IS like a person riding in a boat. Although the person prepares the sails, steers the course, and poles the boat along, it is the *boat* which carries him/her, and without which s/he cannot ride. By riding in a boat s/he makes this boat a boat. We must consider this moment. At such a moment, there is nothing but the boat's world. The heavens, the water, and the shore all become the boat's time, which is never the same as the time that is not the boat. By the same token, birth is what I give birth to, and I am what birth makes me.

JOAN STAMBAUGH, *Impermanence Is Buddha-Nature*

IF I AM going to experience 'infinity' at all, it will be in the palm of my hand. I am not going to experience it by wandering around the whole world because that kind of wandering, be it ever so extensive, can never yield any experience of wholeness or totality whatever. Similarly, if I am going to experience 'eternity,' it is going to be in an 'hour' (better, a moment).

JOAN STAMBAUGH, *Impermanence Is Buddha-Nature*

IT IS considered that the old Chinese Zen Masters ... saw everything in nature as interrelated with everything else, and so did not regard some as good and others as bad, or some as superior or higher and others as inferior or lower. This is quite in agreement with modern science also, by which we can say that everything is what it is and where it is because of everything else – and itself.

ERNEST WOOD, *Zen Dictionary*

FEW WILL argue that the old wine of Zen should be presented to the West only in old bottles (East Asian cultural forms). Americans often demand the 'new, improved' version, even in spiritual matters, and there may be some inclination to distil a new wine and package it in new bottles. But the result might no longer be Zen, nor compare in quality to its predecessor. The appropriate response might be to preserve the old wine, let it age even further, and design effective new bottles for it.

BERNARD GLASSMAN, Instructions to the Cook

SOURCES

Anne Bancroft, *Mystics and Sages*, Heinemann, 1976

Anne Bancroft, *Zen: Direct Pointing to Reality*, Thames & Hudson, 1979

Anne Bancroft, *The Luminous Vision*, George Allen & Unwin, 1982

Anne Bancroft, *Spiritual Journey*, Element, 1991

Anne Bancroft, *Women in Search of the Sacred*, Arkana, 1996

Anne Bancroft, *The Buddha Speaks*, Shambhala, 2000

S. Batchelor, *The Faith to Doubt*, Parallax Press, 1990

Perle Besserman, *Crazy Clouds*, Shambhala, 1991

John Blofeld, *The Zen Teaching of Huang Po*, Buddhist Society, 1958

R.H. Blyth, *Zen in English Literature and Oriental Culture*, Hokusaido Press, 1942

Thomas Cleary, *The Original Face*, Grove Press, 1978

Thomas Cleary, *Zen Essence*, Shambhala, 1989

Taisen Deshimaru, *The Zen Way to the Martial Arts*, Rider, 1982

H. Dumoulin, *Zen Enlightenment*, Weatherhill, 1983

K. Durckheim, *The Grace of Zen*, Search Press, 1977

M. Farkas, *The Zen Eye*, Weatherhill, 1993

Frederick Franck, *The Zen of Seeing*, Wildwood House, 1973

L. Friedman, *Meetings with Remarkable Women*, Shambhala, 1987

Bernard Glassman, *Instructions to the Cook*, Bell Tower, 1996
D.E. Harding, *On Having No Head*, Arkana, 1986
Ralph Heatherington, in *Quaker Faith and Practice*, Religious Society of Friends, 1995
Eugen Herrigel, *Zen in the Art of Archery*, Arkana, 1985
A. Huxley, *The Perennial Philosophy*, Chatto & Windus, 1955
Joe Hyams, *Zen in the Martial Arts*, Bantam, 1982
Toshihiko Izutsu, *Toward a Philosophy of Zen Buddhism*, University of Tokyo, 1977
William Johnston, *The Mysticism of the Cloud of Unknowing*, Desclee, 1967
William Johnston, *The Still Point*, Fordham University Press, 1986
P. Kapleau, *The Three Pillars of Zen*, Beacon Press, 1965
Kenneth Kraft, *Zen Tradition and Transition*, Grove Press, 1988
Lu K'uan Yu, *Ch'an and Zen Teaching, Series 1*, Rider, 1960
Lu K'uan Yu, *Ch'an and Zen Teaching, Series 2*, Rider, 1961
G. Kubose, *Zen Koans*, Henry Regnery, 1973
Bruce Lee, *Striking Thoughts*, Turtle, 2000
Trevor Leggett, *A First Zen Reader*, Charles E. Tuttle, 1960
Trevor Leggett, *Fingers and Moons*, Buddhist Publishing Group, 1988
Trevor Leggett, *The Old Zen Master*, Buddhist Publishing Group, 2000

R. Masanuga, *The Standpoint of Dogen and His Treatise on Time*, University of Tokyo, 1951

Ch'an Master Sheng-Yen, *The Poetry of Enlightenment*, Dharma Drum Publications, 1987

Reiho Masunaga, *A Primer of Soto Zen*, Routledge & Kegan Paul, 1972

Thomas Merton, *Mystics and Zen Masters*, Dell, 1961

D.G. Merzel, *The Eye Never Sleeps*, Shambhala, 1991

Thich Nhat Hahn, *Being Peace*, Parallax Press, 1987

Thich Nhat Hahn, *The Heart of Understanding*, Parallax Press, 1988

Thich Nhat Hanh, *The Sun Is My Heart*, Parallax Press, 1988

Thich Nhat Hahn, *The Diamond that Cuts through Illusion*, Parallax Press, 1992

Sohaku Ogata, *Zen for the West*, Greenwood Press, 1959

Paul Reps, *Zen Flesh, Zen Bones*, Penguin, 1972

Irmgard Schloegl, *The Wisdom of the Zen Masters*, Sheldon Press, 1975

Nyogen Senzaki, *Buddhism and Zen*, North Point Press, 1987

Nyogen Senzaki, *The Iron Flute*, Charles E. Tuttle, 1964

Ninian Smart, *Background to the Long Search*, BBC, 1977

Robert Sohl, *The Gospel According to Zen*, New America Library, 1970

Joan Stambaugh, *Impermanence Is Buddha-Nature*, University of Hawaii Press, 1990

John Stevens, *One Robe, One Bowl*, Weatherhill, 1977

L. Stryck, *Zen: Poems, Prayers, Sermons, Anecdotes, Interviews*, Doubleday, 1963

D.T. Suzuki, *Essays in Zen Buddhism*, Vol. 2, Luzac, 1933

D.T. Suzuki, *Studies in Zen*, Dell, 1955

D.T. Suzuki, *Zen and Japanese Culture*, Princeton University Press, 1959

D.T. Suzuki, *Manual of Zen Buddhism*, Grove Press, 1960

D.T. Suzuki, *Zen Doctrines of No Mind*, Rider, 1969

D.T. Suzuki, *Studies in the Lankavatara Sutra*, Routledge & Kegan Paul, 1972

Kosho Uchiyama Roshi, *Approach to Zen*, Japan Publications, 1973

Alan Watts, *The Way of Zen*, Penguin, 1957

Alan Watts, *Beyond Theology*, Hodder & Stoughton, 1964

Alan Watts, *Does It Matter?*, Vintage, 1971

Alan Watts, *Behold the Spirit*, Vintage, 1972

Middle Way, Journal of the Buddhist Society, London (quarterly)

Claude Whitmyer, *Mindfulness and Meaningful Work*, Parallax Press, 1994

Ernest Wood, *Zen Dictionary*, Penguin, 1957